MathFlare

Name: _______________________

Class: ___________

Teacher: _______________________

Introduction

As parents and educators, we recognize the pivotal role mathematics plays in shaping a child's academic journey and future success. Yet, the path to mathematical proficiency can often seem daunting, fraught with challenges and complexities. That's where the transformative power of MathFlare Workbooks shine through, illuminating the way forward with clarity, precision, and purpose.

Introducing MathFlare Workbooks – a beacon of guidance, a testament to excellence, and a catalyst for achievement. Crafted with meticulous care and expertise, MathFlare Workbooks stand as paragons of educational excellence, designed to nurture young minds, ignite a passion for learning, and develop a deep-rooted understanding of mathematical concepts.

Picture this: your child eagerly delves into the pages of Mathflare Workbook, greeted by a step-by-step guide illuminated with vivid examples that demystify complex mathematical concepts. With each turn of the page, they embark on a journey of discovery, encountering thoughtfully curated practice questions that reinforce learning and hone problem-solving skills. And when they unveil the answers to those very questions, a sense of accomplishment blossoms within them – a tangible reward for their hard work and dedication.

But MathFlare Workbooks are more than just tools for learning; they are pathways to comprehension, fostering a deep-seated understanding of mathematical concepts through a sequential, logical flow. From fundamental principles to advanced problem-solving strategies, every chapter builds upon the last, ensuring a robust foundation upon which future knowledge can be constructed.

As parents, we yearn for nothing more than to see our children thrive, to witness the spark of inspiration ignited within them as they conquer academic challenges with confidence and poise. MathFlare Workbooks serve as partners in this noble endeavor, offering not just practice questions, but the keys to unlocking a world of opportunity.

And for teachers, MathFlare Workbooks stand as invaluable allies in the quest to cultivate mathematical proficiency in the classroom. With answers readily available, instructors can focus on guiding and nurturing their students, confident in the knowledge that MathFlare Workbooks provide a solid framework upon which to build.

In the pages of MathFlare Workbooks, we find not just the promise of academic excellence, but the seeds of a brighter tomorrow. So let us embrace the power of mathematics, let us champion the journey of learning, and let us pave the way for a generation of young minds poised to shape the world. With MathFlare Workbooks as our guide, the possibilities are infinite, and the future, bright.

Table of Contents

MathFlare
MATH WORKBOOK
Grade 2
Step by Step Guide and Essential Practice with Answers
Addition Subtraction
Multiplication
Place Value and Expanded Notations
Geometry
MathFlare Publishing

MathFlare
MATH WORKBOOK
Grade 2-3
Step by Step Guide and Essential Practice with Answers
Addition Subtraction
Multiplication and Division
Place Value and Expanded Notations
Geometry
MathFlare Publishing

MathFlare
MATH WORKBOOK
Grade 3
Step by Step Guide and Essential Practice with Answers
Multiplication and Division
Decimals
Place Value and Expanded Notations
Fractions and Geometry
MathFlare Publishing

MathFlare
MATH WORKBOOK
Grade 1
Step by Step Guide and Essential Practice with Answers
Counting and Numbers
Addition and Subtraction
Place Value and Expanded Notations
Understanding Time
MathFlare Publishing

MathFlare
MATH WORKBOOK
Grade 1-2
Step by Step Guide and Essential Practice with Answers
Counting and Numbers
Addition and Subtraction
Place Value and Expanded Notations
Understanding Time
MathFlare Publishing

MathFlare
MATH WORKBOOK
Grade 3-4
Step by Step Guide and Essential Practice with Answers
Addition Subtraction
Multiplication Division
Place Value and Expanded Notations
Fractions and Geometry
MathFlare Publishing

MathFlare
MATH WORKBOOK
Grade 4
Step by Step Guide and Essential Practice with Answers
Addition Subtraction
Multiplication Division
Place Value and Expanded Notations
Fractions and Geometry
MathFlare Publishing

MathFlare
MATH WORKBOOK
Grade 4-5
Step by Step Guide and Essential Practice with Answers
Multiplication Division
Place Value and Expanded Notations
Fractions and Geometry
Unit Conversion
MathFlare Publishing

MathFlare
MATH WORKBOOK
Grade 5
Step by Step Guide and Essential Practice with Answers
Multiplication Division
Place Value and Expanded Notations
Fractions and Geometry
Unit Conversion
MathFlare Publishing

MathFlare
MATH WORKBOOK
Grade 5-6
Step by Step Guide and Essential Practice with Answers
Multiplication Division
Place Value and Expanded Notations
Fractions and Geometry
Units and Statistics
MathFlare Publishing

MathFlare
MATH WORKBOOK
Grade 6
Step by Step Guide and Essential Practice with Answers
Integers and Statistics
Arithmetic and Pre-Algebra
Fractions and Geometry
Ratio and Percentage
MathFlare Publishing

MathFlare
MATH WORKBOOK
Grade 6-7
Step by Step Guide and Essential Practice with Answers
Arithmetic and Pre-Algebra
Ratio, Percent Proportion
Geometry
Statistics
MathFlare Publishing

MathFlare
MATH WORKBOOK
Grade 7
Step by Step Guide and Essential Practice with Answers
Pre-Algebra
Ratio, Percent Proportion
Geometry
Statistics
MathFlare Publishing

MathFlare
MATH WORKBOOK
Grade 7-8
Step by Step Guide and Essential Practice with Answers
Pre-Algebra
Ratio, Percent Proportion
Geometry and Cartesian Plane
Statistics
MathFlare Publishing

MathFlare
MATH WORKBOOK
Grade 8-9
Step by Step Guide and Essential Practice with Answers
Pre-Algebra
Ratio, Proportion and Percentage
Linear Equations
Geometry and Cartesian Plane
MathFlare Publishing

MathFlare
MATH WORKBOOK
Grade 8
Step by Step Guide and Essential Practice with Answers
Pre-Algebra
Percentage
Linear Equations
Geometry
MathFlare Publishing

Addition and Subtraction

Addition with Regrouping

When we do addition, we combine numbers. But sometimes, when we're adding numbers, we might need to regroup. Regrouping means we have to move a number from one place to another, usually to the next column, to get the right answer.

For Example: Let's take an example of adding 533 and 579 together:

$$5\ 3\ 3$$
$$+\ \underline{5\ 7\ 9}$$

First, we start by adding the digits in the ones place: 3 + 9 = 12. We write down the 2 in the ones place and carry over the 1 to the tens place.

$$1$$
$$5\ 3\ 3$$
$$+\ \underline{5\ 7\ 9}$$
$$2$$

Now, we add the digits in the tens place, along with the carry-over: 2 + 8 + 1 = 11. We write down the 1 in the tens place and carry over the 1 to the hundreds place.

$$1\ 1$$
$$5\ 2\ 2$$
$$+\ \underline{5\ 8\ 9}$$
$$1\ 2$$

Now, we add the digits in the hundreds place, along with the carry-over: 5 + 5 + 1 = 11. We write down the 1 in the tens place and carry over the 1 to the hundreds place.

$$
\begin{array}{r}
1\;1 \\
5\;2\;2 \\
+\;5\;8\;9 \\
\hline
1\,1\,1\,2
\end{array}
$$

This process of carrying over helps us accurately add numbers, especially when they're larger.

Subtraction with Regrouping

Subtraction is a key math operation where we find the difference between two numbers. Sometimes, when we subtract, we might need to regroup, which means borrowing from the next column.

Let's take an example of subtracting 436 from 563:

First, we start by subtracting the digits in the ones place: 3 - 6.

Since 3 is less than 6, we need to regroup. We borrow 1 from the tens place, making it 5 tens instead of 6, and add it to the ones place.

So, 3 becomes 13, and then we subtract 6.

$$
\begin{array}{r}
5\;\;6\;13 \\
-\;4\;\;3\;\;6 \\
\hline
7
\end{array}
$$

Now, we subtract the tens place digits: 5 - 3 = 2

$$
\begin{array}{r}
5 \\
5\;\;\cancel{6}\,13 \\
-\;4\;\;3\;\;6 \\
\hline
2\;\;7
\end{array}
$$

Now, we subtract the hundreds place digits: 5 - 4 = 1

$$
\begin{array}{r}
5 \\
5\ \ \cancel{6}\ \ 13 \\
-\ 4\ \ 3\ \ 6 \\
\hline
1\ \ 2\ \ 7
\end{array}
$$

This process of regrouping or borrowing helps us accurately subtract numbers, especially when the top digit is smaller than the bottom one.

Let's solve problems from exercises:

$$
\begin{array}{r}
714 \\
+\ 797 \\
\hline
1{,}511
\end{array}
\qquad
\begin{array}{r}
980 \\
-\ 896 \\
\hline
84
\end{array}
$$

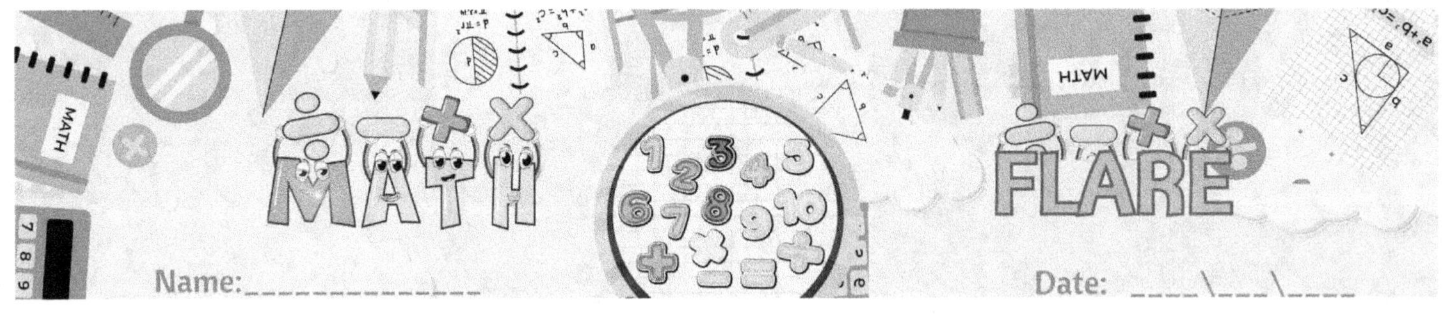

Addition with Regrouping

Find the sum.

1.   816
   + 494
   ———

2.   985
   + 545
   ———

3.   939
   + 189
   ———

4.   544
   + 766
   ———

5.   315
   + 998
   ———

6.   221
   + 889
   ———

7.   215
   + 898
   ———

8.   849
   + 996
   ———

9.   486
   + 765
   ———

10.   127
   + 996
   ———

11.   443
   + 867
   ———

12.   249
   + 869
   ———

13.   948
   + 174
   ———

14.   412
   + 999
   ———

15.   319
   + 796
   ———

16.   149
   + 986
   ———

17.   928
   + 984
   ———

18.   639
   + 599
   ———

19.   869
   + 967
   ———

20.   556
   + 889
   ———

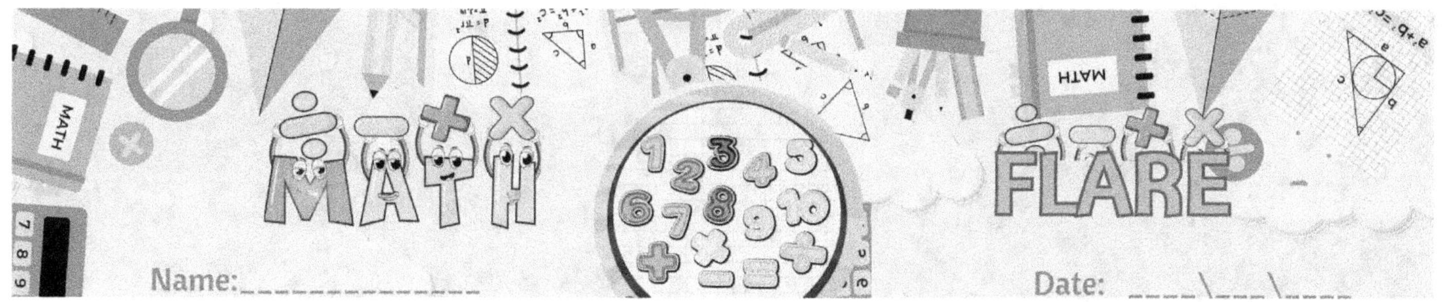

21. 653 + 459	22. 639 + 681	23. 299 + 942	24. 461 + 959
25. 928 + 689	26. 156 + 997	27. 829 + 687	28. 666 + 444
29. 325 + 886	30. 596 + 926	31. 756 + 599	32. 816 + 598
33. 944 + 878	34. 257 + 876	35. 932 + 779	36. 227 + 885
37. 311 + 899	38. 294 + 988	39. 862 + 598	40. 661 + 949

41. 652 + 468	42. 614 + 698	43. 741 + 669	44. 586 + 624
45. 338 + 975	46. 913 + 797	47. 414 + 699	48. 527 + 688
49. 448 + 793	50. 716 + 494	51. 586 + 859	52. 114 + 997
53. 513 + 599	54. 287 + 985	55. 434 + 678	56. 551 + 799
57. 566 + 899	58. 374 + 796	59. 517 + 598	60. 777 + 399

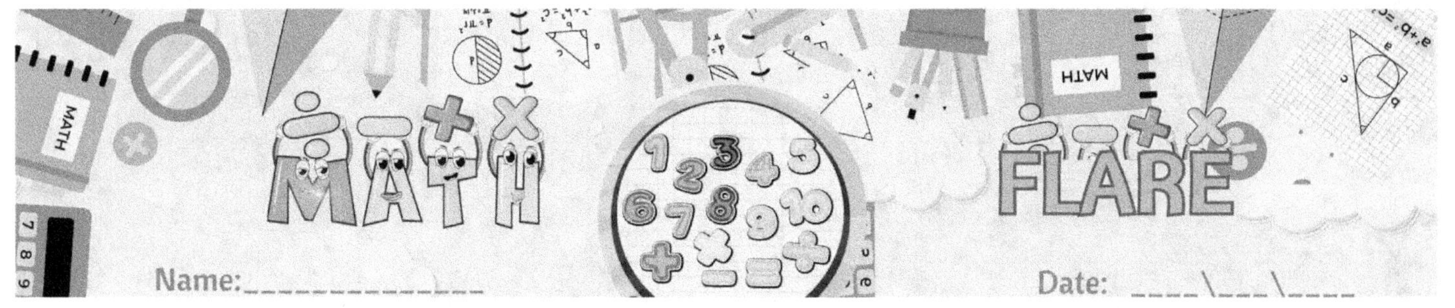

61. 317 + 895	62. 972 + 738	63. 817 + 493	64. 281 + 889
65. 417 + 699	66. 839 + 772	67. 889 + 265	68. 719 + 592
69. 462 + 998	70. 276 + 877	71. 464 + 697	72. 966 + 859
73. 774 + 776	74. 277 + 964	75. 355 + 876	76. 234 + 976
77. 443 + 667	78. 277 + 936	79. 277 + 996	80. 489 + 722

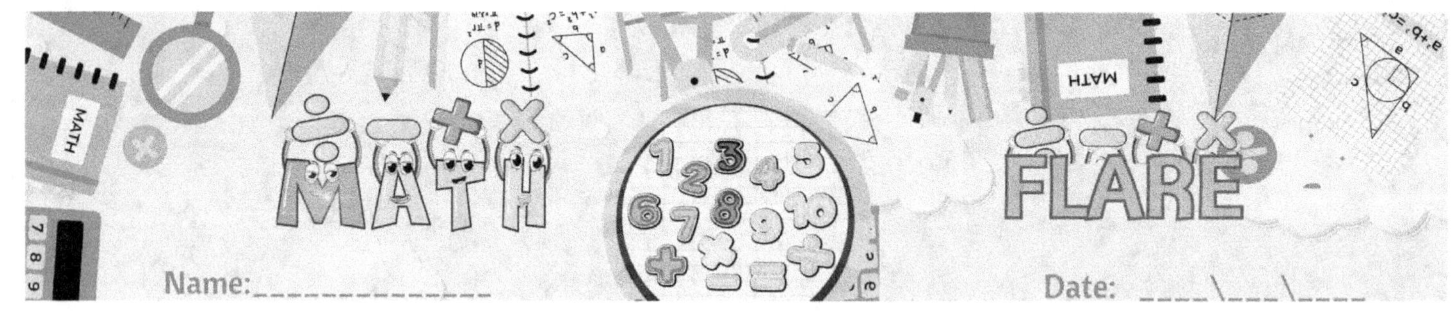

81. 389 + 846	82. 668 + 787	83. 638 + 878	84. 837 + 489
85. 671 + 879	86. 927 + 288	87. 951 + 669	88. 927 + 796
89. 888 + 243	90. 932 + 688	91. 315 + 996	92. 425 + 889
93. 518 + 699	94. 399 + 875	95. 987 + 988	96. 324 + 986
97. 917 + 296	98. 881 + 859	99. 931 + 289	100. 321 + 989

Subtraction with Regrouping

Find the difference.

101. 230 − 194	102. 948 − 159	103. 301 − 225	104. 503 − 119
105. 877 − 599	106. 265 − 177	107. 237 − 159	108. 975 − 587
109. 884 − 797	110. 611 − 358	111. 574 − 396	112. 245 − 157
113. 412 − 129	114. 466 − 287	115. 983 − 498	116. 526 − 167
117. 201 − 185	118. 956 − 867	119. 216 − 179	120. 375 − 287

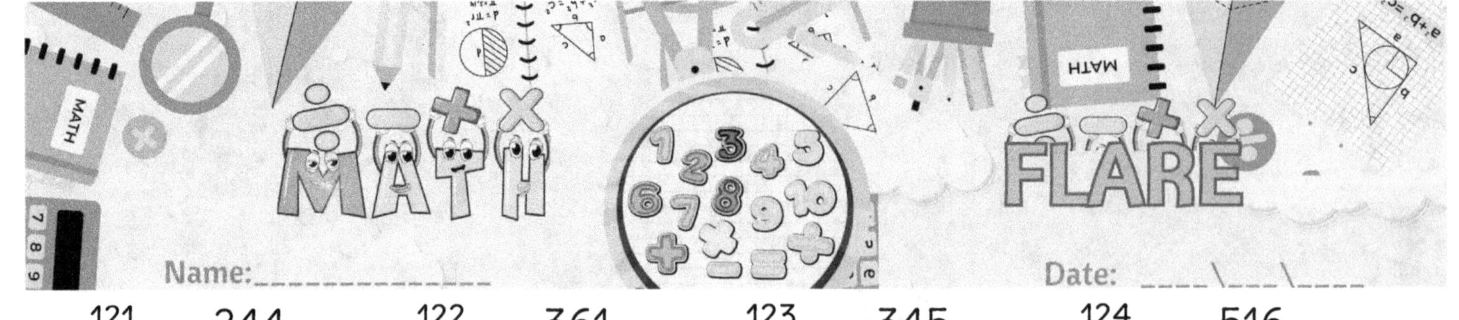

121. $244 - 199$	122. $361 - 185$	123. $345 - 199$	124. $516 - 449$
125. $548 - 159$	126. $408 - 369$	127. $240 - 159$	128. $938 - 559$
129. $776 - 587$	130. $732 - 188$	131. $268 - 189$	132. $248 - 199$
133. $274 - 197$	134. $238 - 169$	135. $767 - 199$	136. $433 - 167$
137. $703 - 528$	138. $410 - 369$	139. $385 - 298$	140. $955 - 876$

141.	142.	143.	144.
667 - 499	937 - 869	231 - 199	986 - 798

145.	146.	147.	148.
652 - 369	218 - 149	981 - 197	715 - 188

149.	150.	151.	152.
671 - 599	320 - 151	488 - 399	274 - 185

153.	154.	155.	156.
782 - 198	263 - 175	942 - 186	386 - 199

157.	158.	159.	160.
781 - 695	548 - 379	278 - 199	506 - 287

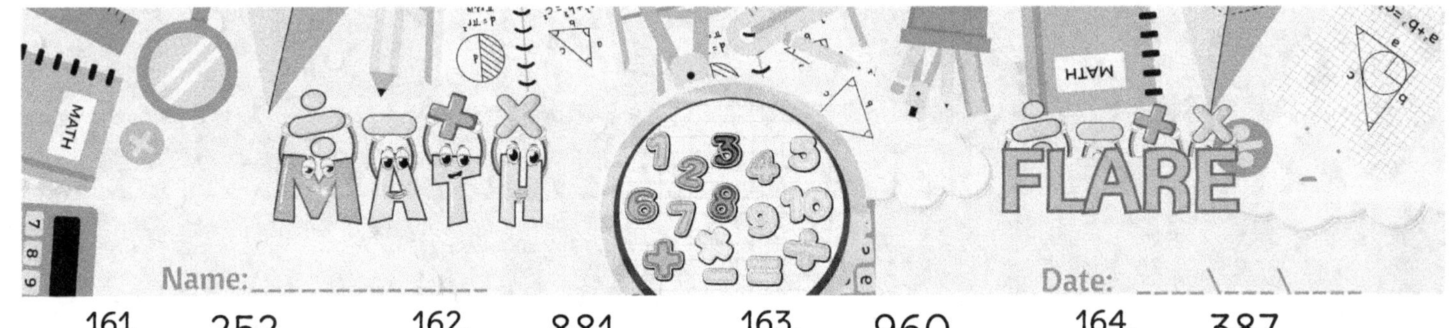

161. 252 − 177	162. 881 − 398	163. 960 − 886	164. 387 − 299
165. 212 − 174	166. 283 − 199	167. 528 − 449	168. 675 − 488
169. 550 − 374	170. 286 − 198	171. 487 − 399	172. 804 − 466
173. 277 − 188	174. 676 − 287	175. 608 − 149	176. 250 − 172
177. 417 − 349	178. 255 − 169	179. 280 − 191	180. 508 − 429

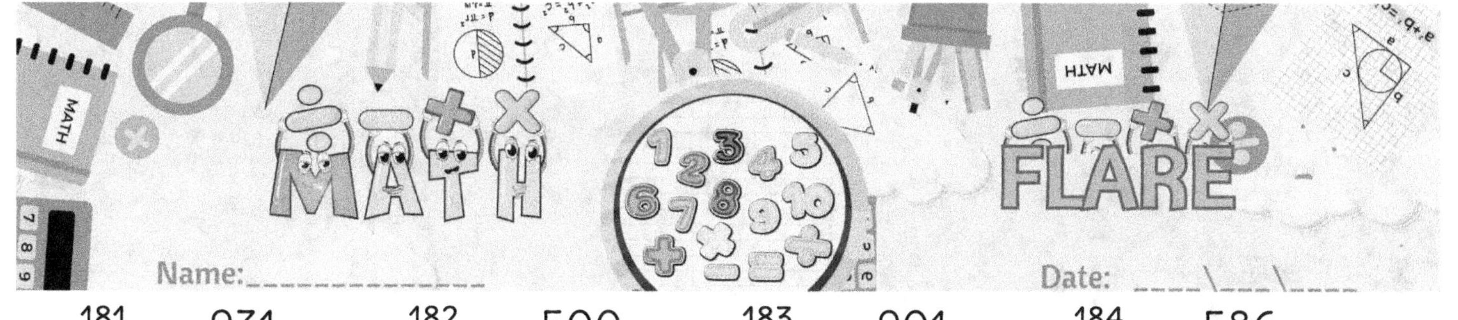

Name:_________________ Date: _______________

181. 931 − 578	182. 500 − 394	183. 901 − 843	184. 586 − 199
185. 282 − 199	186. 284 − 198	187. 217 − 179	188. 585 − 296
189. 316 − 287	190. 236 − 149	191. 244 − 197	192. 583 − 496
193. 615 − 486	194. 260 − 189	195. 968 − 889	196. 274 − 187
197. 665 − 189	198. 585 − 396	199. 341 − 273	200. 975 − 588

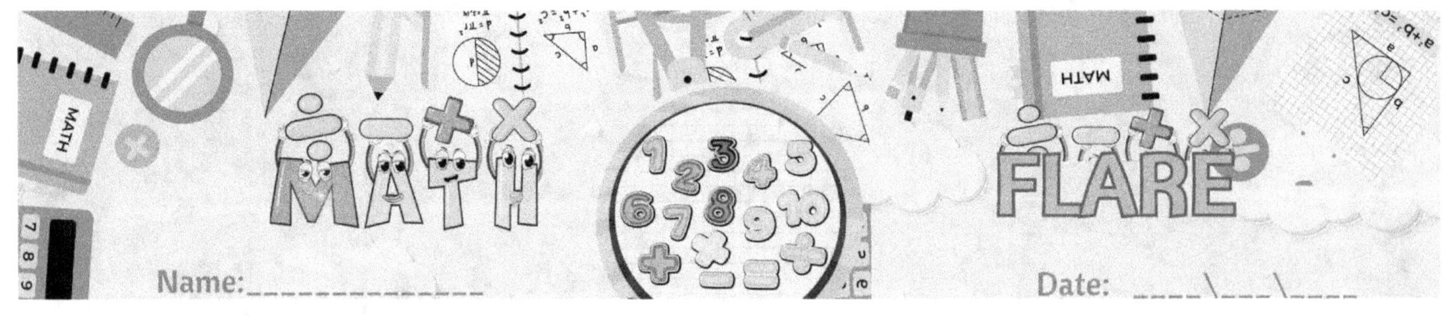

Addition - Doubles

Find the sum.

201. 748 + 749	202. 787 + 785	203. 297 + 296	204. 324 + 326
205. 112 + 112	206. 425 + 423	207. 940 + 940	208. 755 + 753
209. 394 + 393	210. 747 + 749	211. 419 + 420	212. 824 + 823
213. 761 + 762	214. 536 + 534	215. 639 + 639	216. 196 + 196
217. 706 + 706	218. 859 + 859	219. 565 + 567	220. 640 + 642

221. 128 + 129	222. 768 + 770	223. 195 + 196	224. 205 + 203
225. 192 + 194	226. 436 + 438	227. 419 + 419	228. 212 + 212
229. 850 + 851	230. 576 + 575	231. 471 + 472	232. 466 + 466
233. 591 + 593	234. 433 + 432	235. 840 + 842	236. 786 + 788
237. 283 + 282	238. 512 + 511	239. 606 + 607	240. 442 + 441

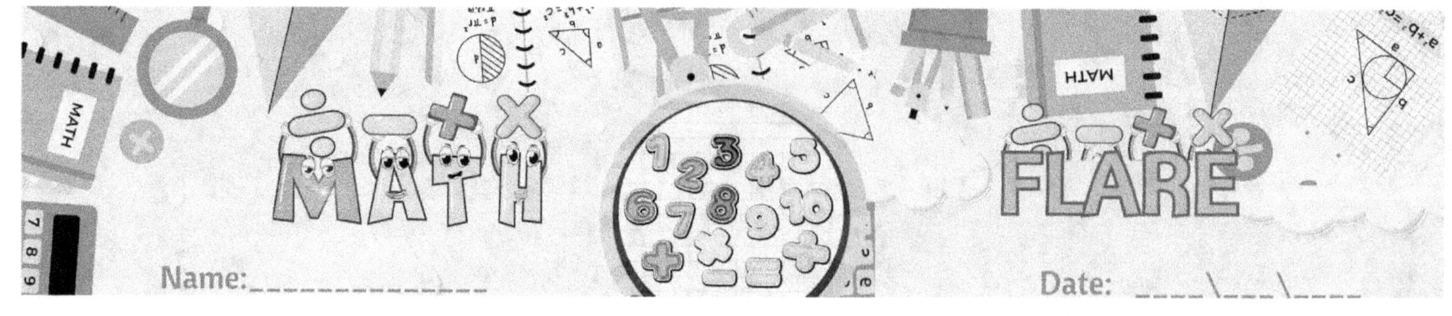

241. 579 + 579	242. 995 + 996	243. 677 + 675	244. 107 + 105
245. 183 + 184	246. 460 + 459	247. 168 + 168	248. 454 + 456
249. 108 + 106	250. 330 + 332	251. 174 + 173	252. 184 + 183
253. 993 + 995	254. 640 + 640	255. 865 + 866	256. 907 + 908
257. 135 + 136	258. 240 + 242	259. 426 + 424	260. 533 + 531

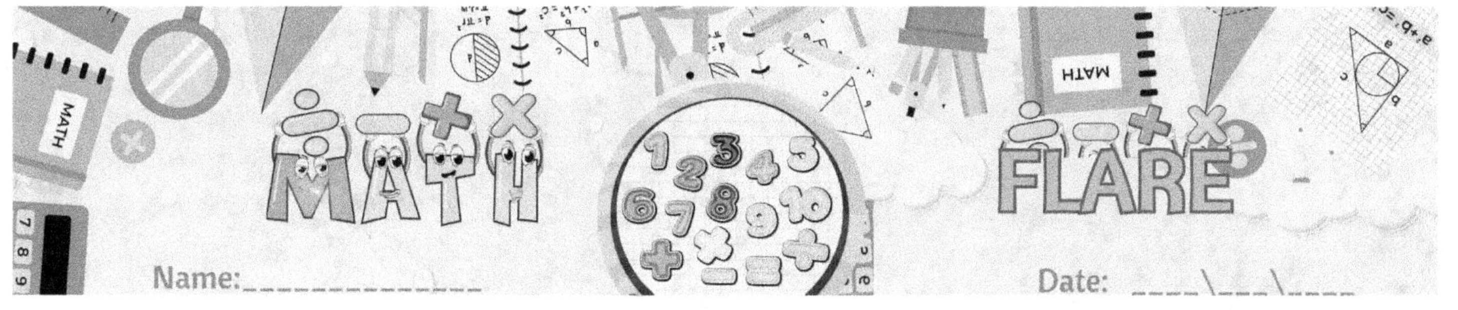

261. 819 + 817	262. 738 + 737	263. 998 + 999	264. 239 + 239
265. 245 + 246	266. 319 + 321	267. 868 + 869	268. 547 + 546
269. 687 + 685	270. 927 + 925	271. 117 + 115	272. 621 + 622
273. 409 + 410	274. 990 + 992	275. 753 + 752	276. 447 + 445
277. 446 + 445	278. 560 + 561	279. 635 + 633	280. 978 + 979

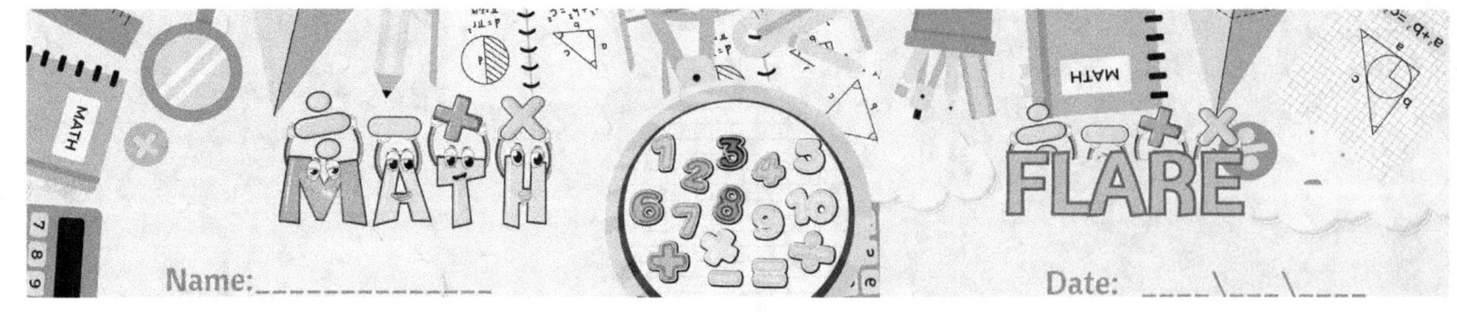

281. 972 + 974 ———	282. 468 + 468 ———	283. 404 + 404 ———	284. 609 + 608 ———
285. 404 + 406 ———	286. 111 + 112 ———	287. 747 + 745 ———	288. 761 + 763 ———
289. 832 + 831 ———	290. 260 + 260 ———	291. 266 + 266 ———	292. 866 + 868 ———
293. 492 + 493 ———	294. 219 + 221 ———	295. 740 + 739 ———	296. 190 + 192 ———
297. 718 + 718 ———	298. 701 + 701 ———	299. 124 + 126 ———	300. 253 + 254 ———

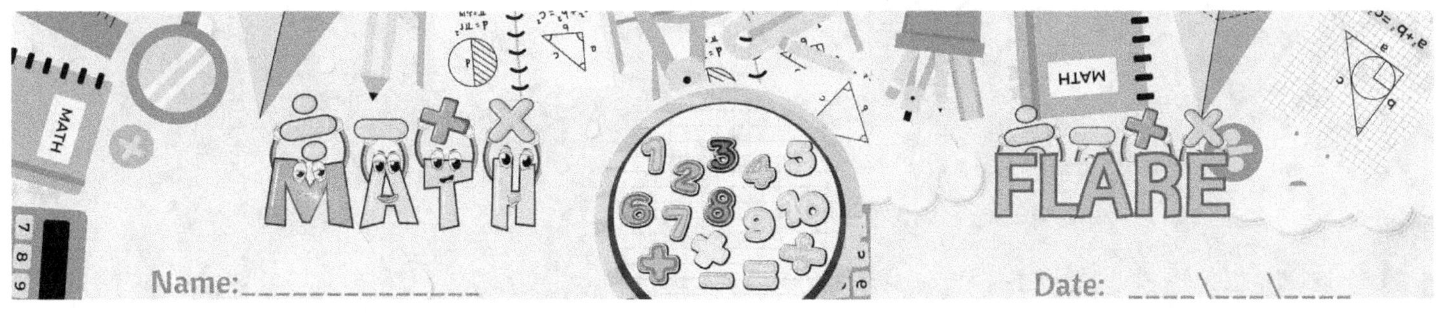

Addition Unknown Number

Find the unknown number.

301. $52 + \underline{\quad} = 140$

302. $\underline{\quad} + 96 = 110$

303. $79 + \underline{\quad} = 154$

304. $72 + \underline{\quad} = 120$

305. $\underline{\quad} + 99 = 110$

306. $51 + \underline{\quad} = 110$

307. $\underline{\quad} + 38 = 131$

308. $65 + 7 = \underline{\quad}$

309. $\underline{\quad} + 86 = 152$

310. $53 + 69 = \underline{\quad}$

311. $9 + 66 = \underline{\quad}$

312. $97 + 57 = \underline{\quad}$

313. $22 + 99 = \underline{\quad}$

314. $66 + 95 = \underline{\quad}$

315. $\underline{\quad} + 98 = 142$

316. $23 + 87 = \underline{\quad}$

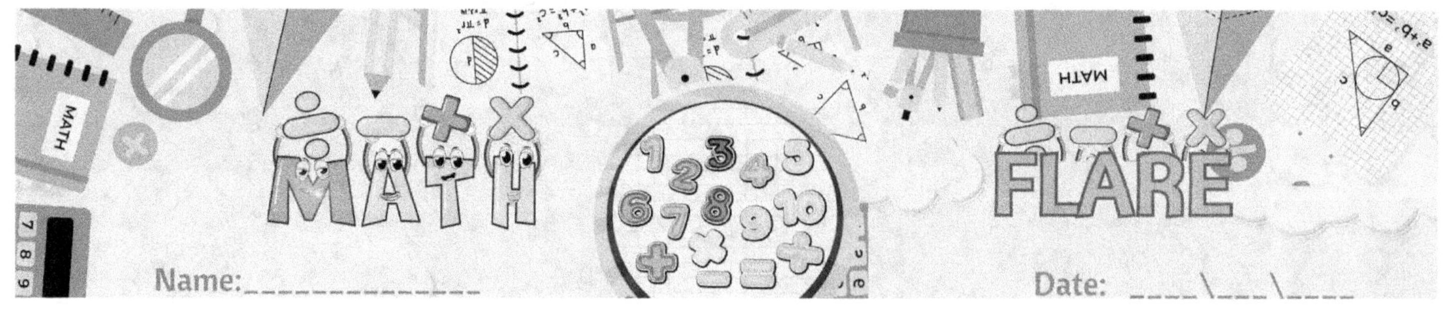

317. _____ + 99 = 116

318. 31 + _____ = 130

319. 71 + 79 = _____

320. 41 + 89 = _____

321. 77 + _____ = 143

322. 26 + _____ = 121

323. _____ + 5 = 14

324. 26 + 88 = _____

325. 27 + 93 = _____

326. _____ + 89 = 150

327. _____ + 65 = 111

328. 65 + 86 = _____

329. _____ + 64 = 130

330. 33 + 79 = _____

331. 8 + _____ = 23

332. 98 + 55 = _____

333. _____ + 87 = 116

334. 73 + _____ = 111

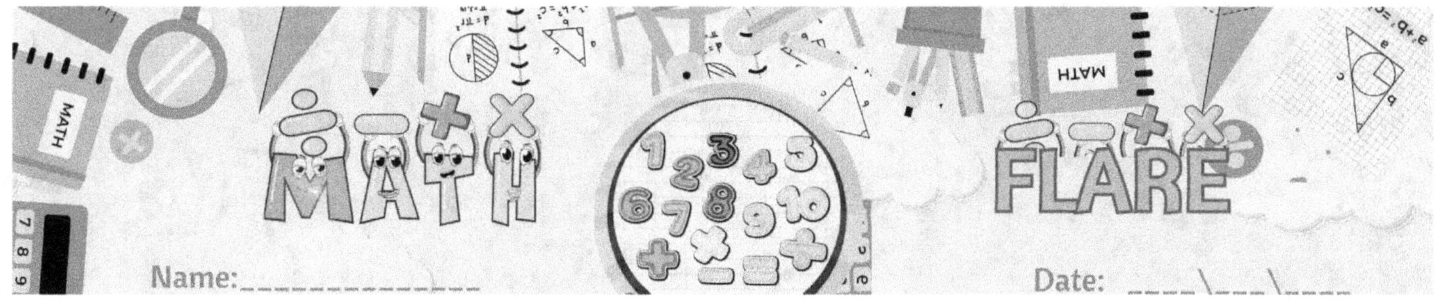

335. 79 + 53 = _____

336. 89 + 31 = _____

337. 32 + 99 = _____

338. _____ + 87 = 131

339. 87 + 49 = _____

340. 69 + _____ = 143

341. 54 + 87 = _____

342. _____ + 99 = 120

343. _____ + 46 = 111

344. 16 + 96 = _____

345. 88 + _____ = 152

346. _____ + 86 = 120

347. 5 + 95 = _____

348. 45 + _____ = 111

349. 74 + 39 = _____

350. 74 + _____ = 171

351. _____ + 8 = 22

352. 95 + 15 = _____

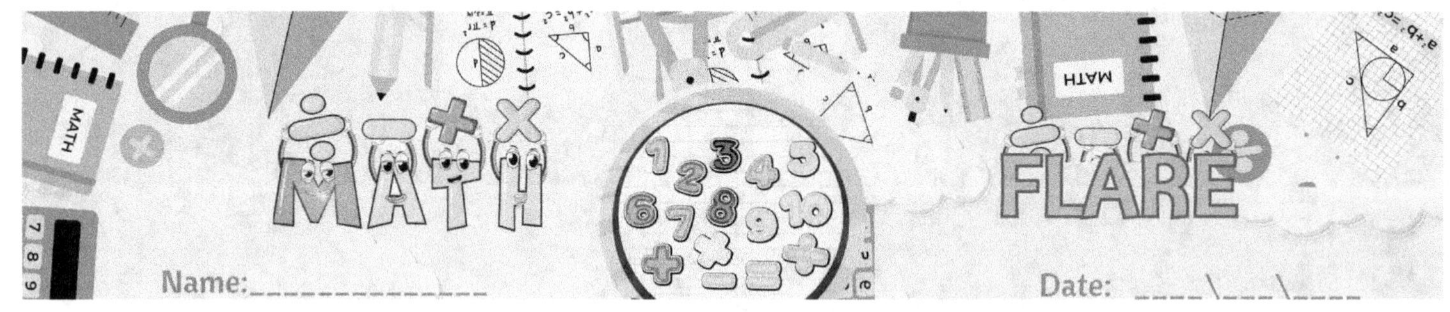

353. 24 + 96 = ____

354. 81 + 89 = ____

355. 88 + 26 = ____

356. ____ + 99 = 115

357. ____ + 58 = 152

358. 91 + 19 = ____

359. 74 + 89 = ____

360. ____ + 97 = 112

361. 97 + ____ = 173

362. ____ + 49 = 56

363. 77 + ____ = 112

364. ____ + 78 = 143

365. ____ + 57 = 156

366. ____ + 99 = 111

367. 92 + ____ = 150

368. 4 + ____ = 32

369. ____ + 69 = 142

370. ____ + 89 = 110

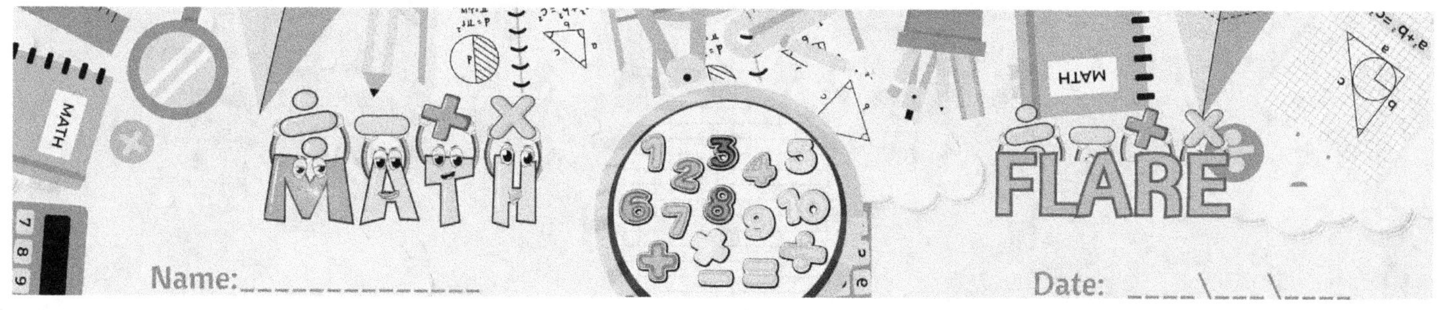

371. _____ + 79 = 120

372. _____ + 99 = 100

373. 63 + 67 = _____

374. _____ + 89 = 153

375. 82 + 99 = _____

376. 42 + _____ = 120

377. _____ + 97 = 115

378. 51 + _____ = 120

379. _____ + 79 = 140

380. 59 + 58 = _____

381. _____ + 89 = 160

382. 5 + _____ = 54

383. _____ + 86 = 172

384. 43 + 8 = _____

385. 6 + _____ = 33

386. 36 + _____ = 124

387. 49 + 86 = _____

388. 71 + _____ = 80

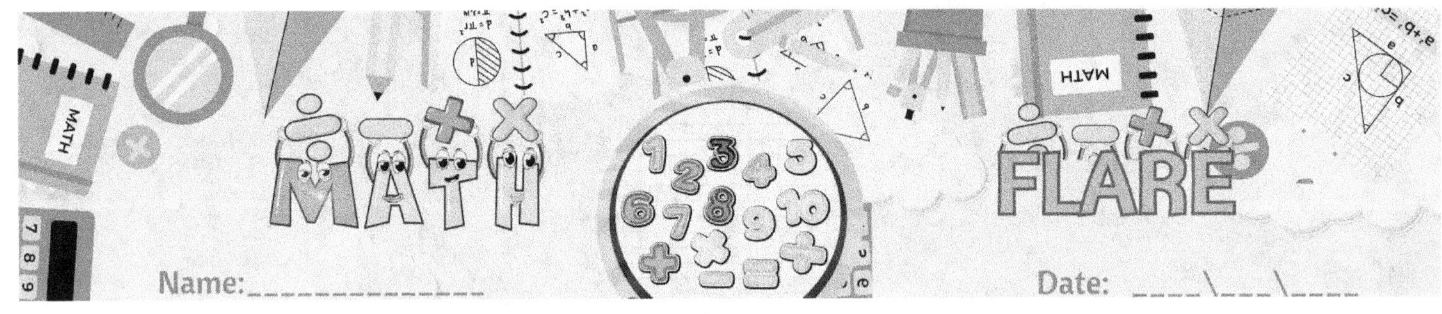

Subtraction: Unknown Number

Find the unknown number.

389. 71 - ___ = 43

390. 34 - 24 = ___

391. ___ - 17 = 79

392. 76 - ___ = 53

393. 82 - 27 = ___

394. 84 - 57 = ___

395. 90 - ___ = 22

396. ___ - 18 = 33

397. 78 - 51 = ___

398. 51 - 23 = ___

399. ___ - 42 = 47

400. 85 - ___ = 53

401. 42 - 41 = ___

402. 75 - ___ = 59

403. 68 - ___ = 33

404. ___ - 21 = 0

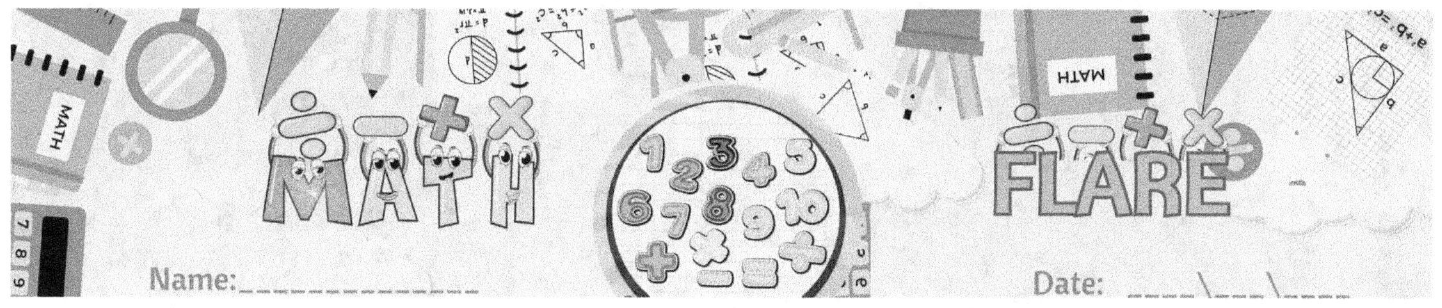

405. 74 - ___ = 56

406. ___ - 45 = 9

407. ___ - 10 = 10

408. 59 - 10 = ___

409. 59 - ___ = 35

410. 89 - ___ = 35

411. ___ - 40 = 18

412. 24 - 12 = ___

413. ___ - 23 = 0

414. 41 - 41 = ___

415. 98 - 96 = ___

416. ___ - 34 = 61

417. ___ - 48 = 1

418. 31 - ___ = 0

419. ___ - 30 = 11

420. 59 - 29 = ___

421. 20 - ___ = 1

422. ___ - 73 = 18

423. ___ - 24 = 7

424. 19 - 17 = ___

425. 15 - ___ = 3

426. 79 - 52 = ___

427. 57 - 24 = ___

428. 77 - 59 = ___

429. ___ - 54 = 29

430. 94 - ___ = 28

431. 17 - 11 = ___

432. ___ - 75 = 23

433. ___ - 13 = 12

434. ___ - 14 = 27

435. 79 - ___ = 31

436. 69 - ___ = 6

437. ___ - 43 = 33

438. 50 - 37 = ___

439. 74 - ___ = 39

440. 90 - 48 = ___

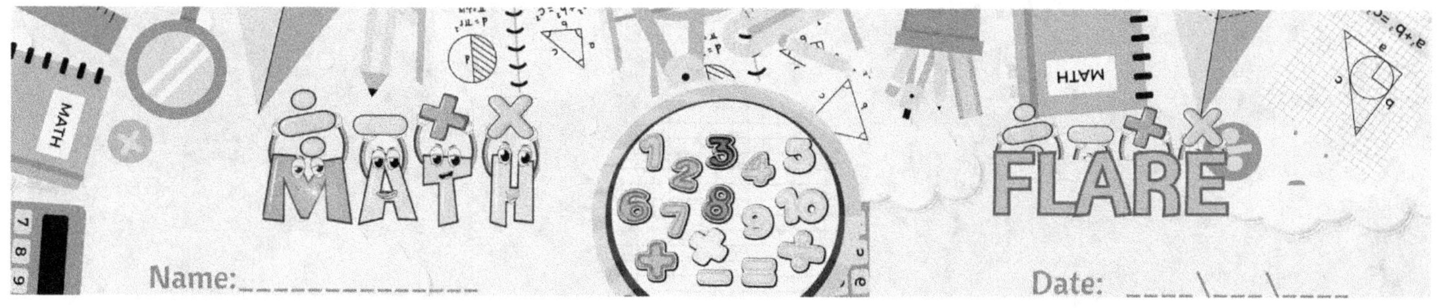

441. 89 - ___ = 32

442. 94 - ___ = 39

443. ___ - 16 = 12

444. 77 - 20 = ___

445. 31 - 20 = ___

446. 25 - ___ = 4

447. ___ - 65 = 7

448. ___ - 38 = 0

449. ___ - 23 = 64

450. 64 - ___ = 53

451. ___ - 38 = 1

452. ___ - 54 = 43

453. 80 - 71 = ___

454. ___ - 12 = 75

455. 85 - 15 = ___

456. 11 - 10 = ___

457. 72 - ___ = 33

458. 79 - 43 = ___

459. 27 - 18 = ___

460. 58 - 49 = ___

461. 89 - ___ = 57

462. 44 - ___ = 3

463. 28 - ___ = 3

464. 82 - 50 = ___

465. 79 - 71 = ___

466. 23 - 22 = ___

467. 65 - ___ = 31

468. 76 - 32 = ___

469. ___ - 42 = 11

470. ___ - 15 = 23

471. ___ - 41 = 12

472. ___ - 11 = 4

473. ___ - 18 = 2

474. ___ - 40 = 41

475. ___ - 54 = 12

476. 59 - 17 = ___

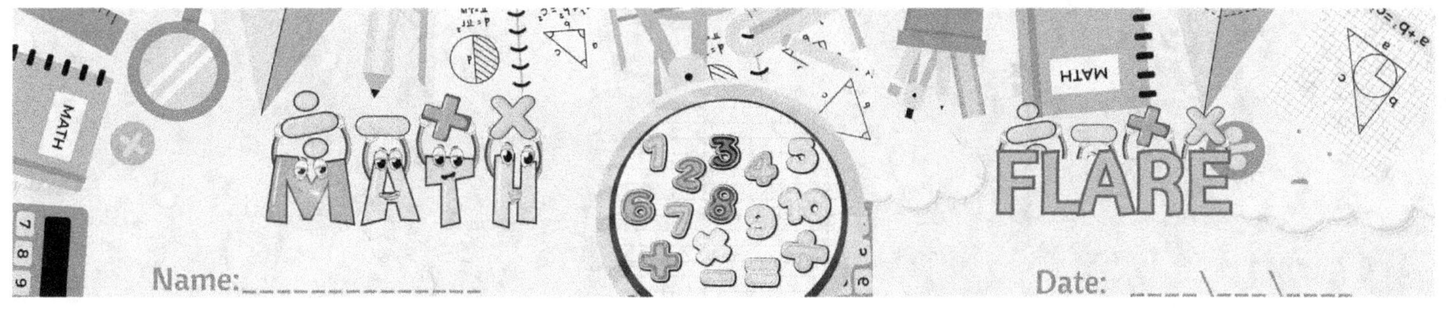

Make 1000

Add a number to the first number to make 1000.

477. 691 + _____ = 1,000

478. 885 + _____ = 1,000

479. 5 + _____ = 1,000

480. 378 + _____ = 1,000

481. 458 + _____ = 1,000

482. 805 + _____ = 1,000

483. 853 + _____ = 1,000

484. 750 + _____ = 1,000

485. 214 + _____ = 1,000

486. 727 + _____ = 1,000

487. 711 + _____ = 1,000

488. 657 + _____ = 1,000

489. 986 + _____ = 1,000

490. 352 + _____ = 1,000

491. 394 + _____ = 1,000

492. 990 + _____ = 1,000

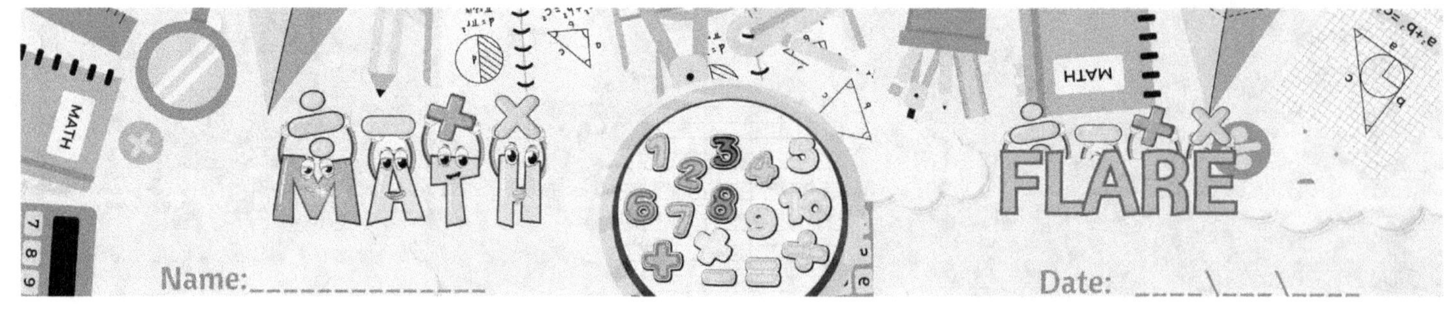

493. 4 + ____ = 1,000

494. 929 + ___ = 1,000

495. 858 + ____ = 1,000

496. 481 + ____ = 1,000

497. 936 + ___ = 1,000

498. 26 + ____ = 1,000

499. 255 + ____ = 1,000

500. 257 + ____ = 1,000

501. 49 + ____ = 1,000

502. 411 + ____ = 1,000

503. 824 + ____ = 1,000

504. 680 + ____ = 1,000

505. 482 + ____ = 1,000

506. 859 + ___ = 1,000

507. 672 + ____ = 1,000

508. 330 + ____ = 1,000

509. 926 + ___ = 1,000

510. 850 + ____ = 1,000

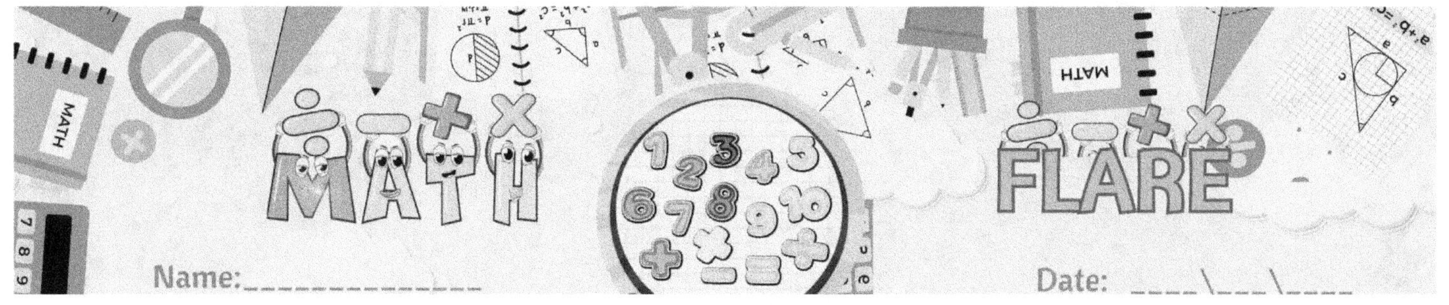

511. 856 + ____ = 1,000

512. 937 + ____ = 1,000

513. 776 + ____ = 1,000

514. 591 + ____ = 1,000

515. 493 + ____ = 1,000

516. 614 + ____ = 1,000

517. 521 + ____ = 1,000

518. 511 + ____ = 1,000

519. 452 + ____ = 1,000

520. 861 + ____ = 1,000

521. 979 + ____ = 1,000

522. 418 + ____ = 1,000

523. 60 + ____ = 1,000

524. 395 + ____ = 1,000

525. 559 + ____ = 1,000

526. 52 + ____ = 1,000

527. 328 + ____ = 1,000

528. 114 + ____ = 1,000

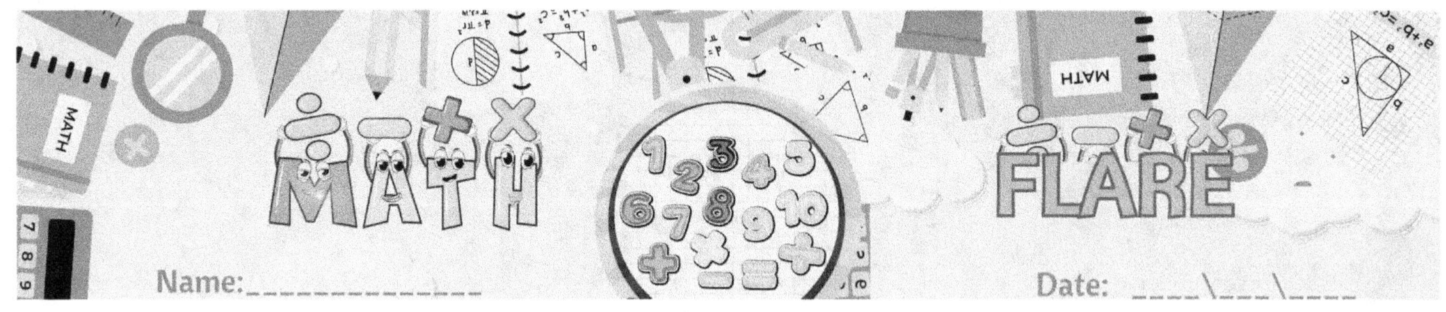

529. 448 + _____ = 1,000

530. 762 + _____ = 1,000

531. 102 + _____ = 1,000

532. 6 + _____ = 1,000

533. 957 + _____ = 1,000

534. 573 + _____ = 1,000

535. 569 + _____ = 1,000

536. 572 + _____ = 1,000

537. 733 + _____ = 1,000

538. 196 + _____ = 1,000

539. 539 + _____ = 1,000

540. 323 + _____ = 1,000

541. 825 + _____ = 1,000

542. 951 + _____ = 1,000

543. 409 + _____ = 1,000

544. 372 + _____ = 1,000

545. 463 + _____ = 1,000

546. 120 + _____ = 1,000

Addition (3 Addends)

Find the sum.

547.
```
   952
   355
 + 903
 ______
```

548.
```
   220
   992
 + 416
 ______
```

549.
```
   543
   579
 + 117
 ______
```

550.
```
   517
   776
 + 670
 ______
```

551.
```
   752
   679
 + 668
 ______
```

552.
```
   307
   639
 + 838
 ______
```

553.
```
   859
   977
 + 753
 ______
```

554.
```
   506
   955
 + 689
 ______
```

555.
```
   335
   241
 + 727
 ______
```

556.
```
   594
   805
 + 727
 ______
```

557.
```
   903
   216
 + 845
 ______
```

558.
```
   526
   449
 + 859
 ______
```

559.
```
   974
   989
 + 152
 ______
```

560.
```
   135
   977
 + 708
 ______
```

561.
```
   176
   343
 + 184
 ______
```

562.
```
   716
   959
 + 282
 ______
```

563.	564.	565.	566.
893 842 + 738	803 248 + 480	991 546 + 399	314 884 + 851

567.	568.	569.	570.
687 948 + 772	388 613 + 660	824 326 + 330	808 332 + 650

571.	572.	573.	574.
786 823 + 101	145 430 + 712	606 618 + 281	546 700 + 963

575.	576.	577.	578.
988 200 + 967	464 534 + 902	560 761 + 204	300 447 + 129

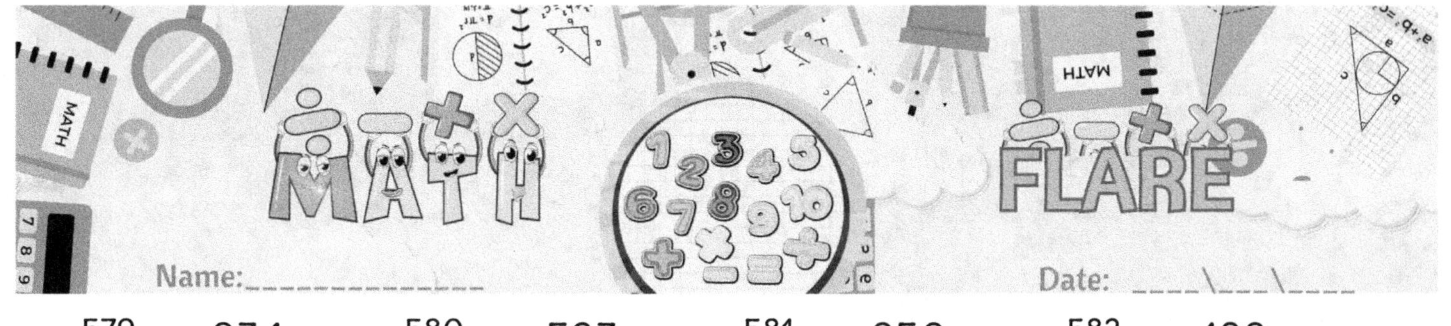

| 579. | 934
787
+ 728 | 580. | 523
890
+ 734 | 581. | 950
185
+ 610 | 582. | 188
116
+ 424 |

| 583. | 480
945
+ 216 | 584. | 686
707
+ 366 | 585. | 670
242
+ 348 | 586. | 809
399
+ 513 |

| 587. | 692
460
+ 790 | 588. | 427
348
+ 570 | 589. | 545
587
+ 476 | 590. | 971
210
+ 642 |

| 591. | 983
183
+ 727 | 592. | 546
594
+ 615 | 593. | 452
901
+ 184 | 594. | 644
984
+ 588 |

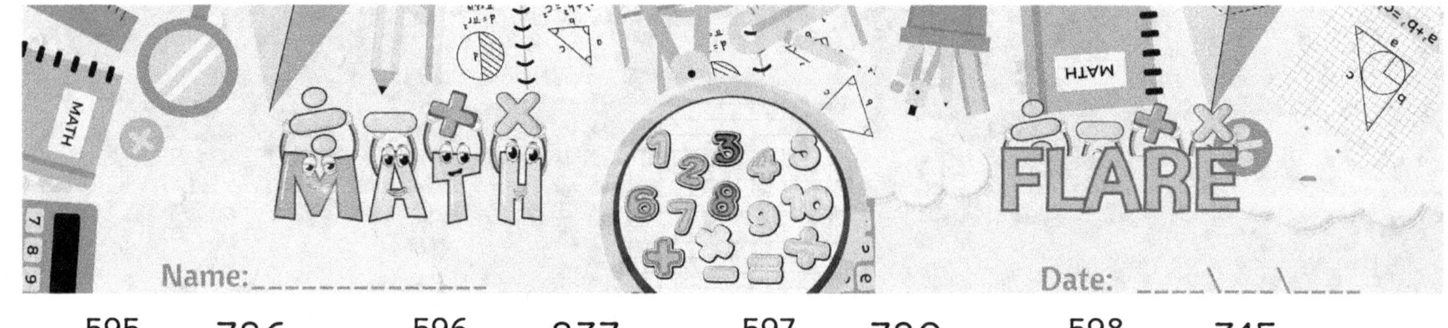

595. 786 872 + 153	596. 837 629 + 306	597. 780 225 + 488	598. 315 830 + 531
599. 942 623 + 836	600. 140 642 + 529	601. 947 508 + 835	602. 573 703 + 624
603. 638 223 + 646	604. 732 456 + 497	605. 429 148 + 475	606. 302 640 + 475
607. 517 707 + 957	608. 271 291 + 984	609. 254 767 + 352	610. 296 603 + 970

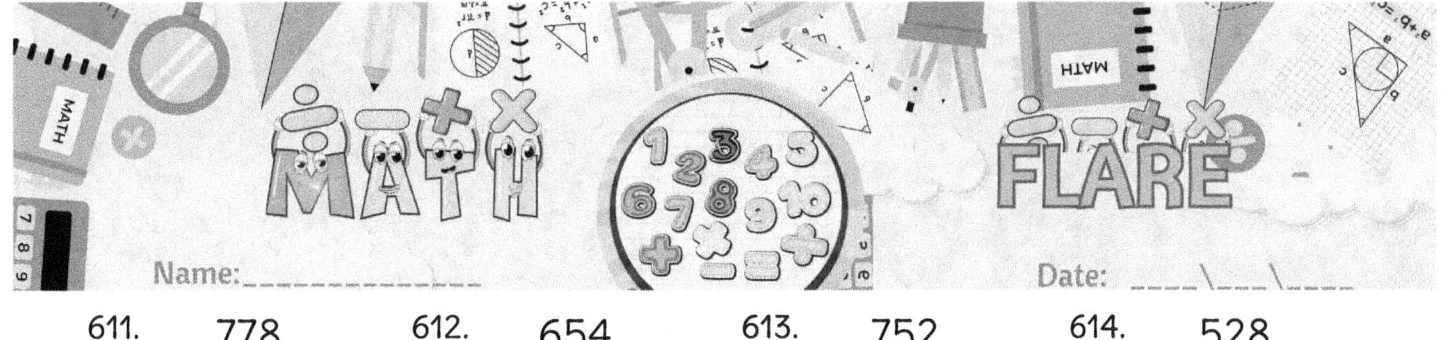

611.   778
      412
+ 359
————
	612. 654
	      696
	+ 576
	————
		613. 752
		      313
		+ 270
		————
			614. 528
			      299
			+ 505
			————

615.   658
      148
+ 768
————
	616. 989
	      885
	+ 782
	————
		617. 155
		      740
		+ 982
		————
			618. 461
			      623
			+ 934
			————

619.   571
      776
+ 317
————
	620. 851
	      419
	+ 934
	————
		621. 373
		      442
		+ 619
		————
			622. 675
			      952
			+ 144
			————

623.   239
      774
+ 451
————
	624. 898
	      549
	+ 427
	————
		625. 305
		      988
		+ 507
		————
			626. 551
			      611
			+ 242
			————

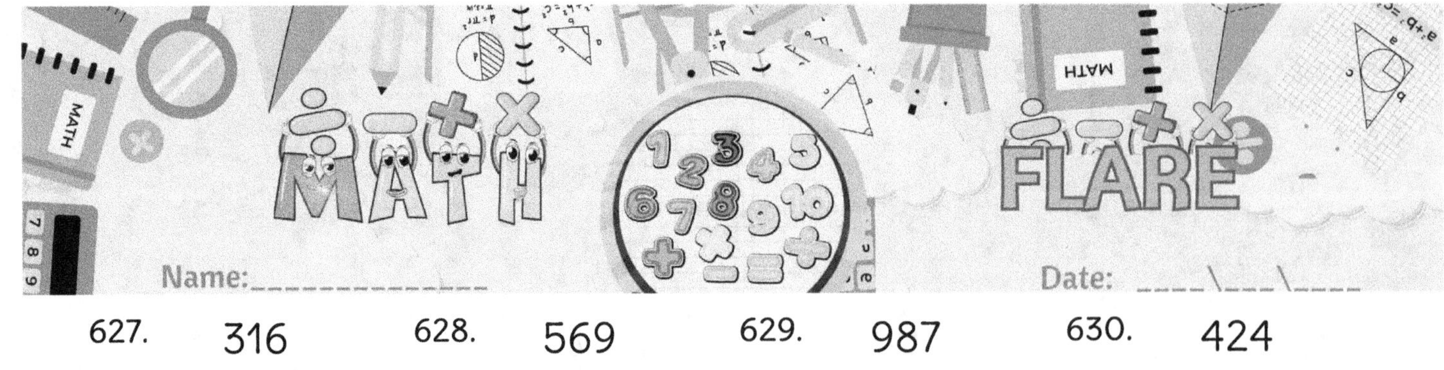

627. 316 264 + 881	628. 569 241 + 862	629. 987 417 + 789	630. 424 183 + 919
631. 359 900 + 893	632. 334 255 + 857	633. 885 982 + 195	634. 724 851 + 211
635. 431 256 + 290	636. 656 256 + 634	637. 526 120 + 265	638. 174 635 + 255
639. 154 803 + 301	640. 756 688 + 635	641. 354 814 + 691	642. 531 639 + 648

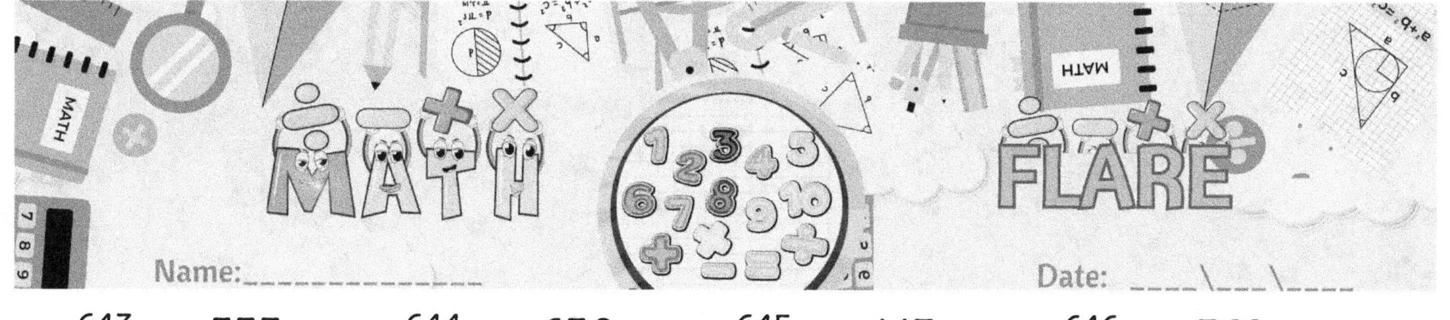

643.
```
   533
   970
+  832
_______
```

644.
```
   650
   665
+  628
_______
```

645.
```
   147
   591
+  412
_______
```

646.
```
   769
   238
+  984
_______
```

647.
```
   672
   431
+  261
_______
```

648.
```
   255
   897
+  163
_______
```

649.
```
   755
   285
+  365
_______
```

650.
```
   738
   281
+  452
_______
```

651.
```
   656
   229
+  395
_______
```

652.
```
   559
   470
+  137
_______
```

653.
```
   520
   899
+  616
_______
```

654.
```
   641
   223
+  285
_______
```

655.
```
   801
   875
+  454
_______
```

656.
```
   636
   127
+  144
_______
```

657.
```
   842
   383
+  665
_______
```

658.
```
   316
   184
+  356
_______
```

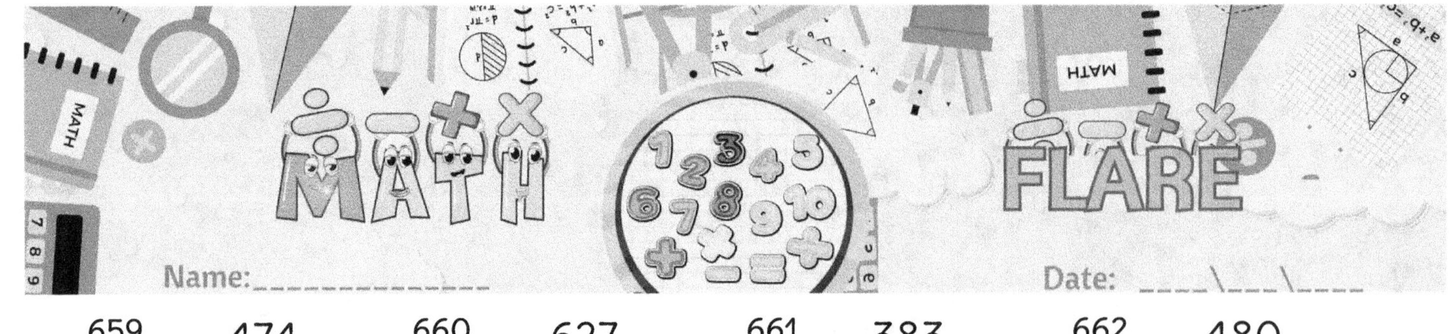

659. 474 200 + 916	660. 627 775 + 454	661. 383 794 + 789	662. 480 993 + 536
663. 333 588 + 221	664. 375 350 + 337	665. 468 130 + 308	666. 976 453 + 121
667. 709 219 + 258	668. 321 894 + 896	669. 786 440 + 146	670. 138 185 + 370
671. 221 891 + 224	672. 262 359 + 428	673. 494 421 + 881	674. 917 402 + 538

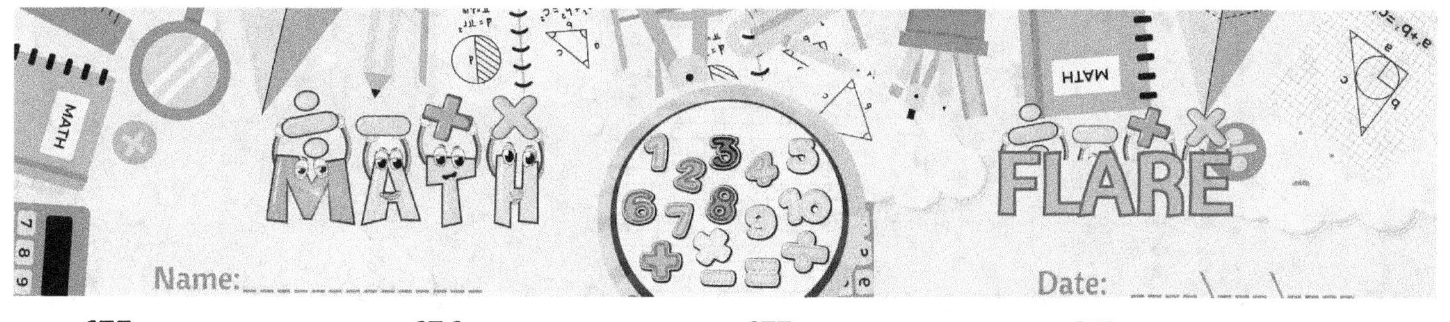

675. 922 568 + 133	676. 427 848 + 153	677. 148 497 + 746	678. 894 918 + 656
679. 296 162 + 898	680. 892 693 + 654	681. 490 295 + 503	682. 850 254 + 458
683. 213 306 + 771	684. 879 581 + 132	685. 239 790 + 816	686. 718 398 + 427
687. 863 459 + 591	688. 991 989 + 687	689. 623 325 + 972	690. 567 965 + 297

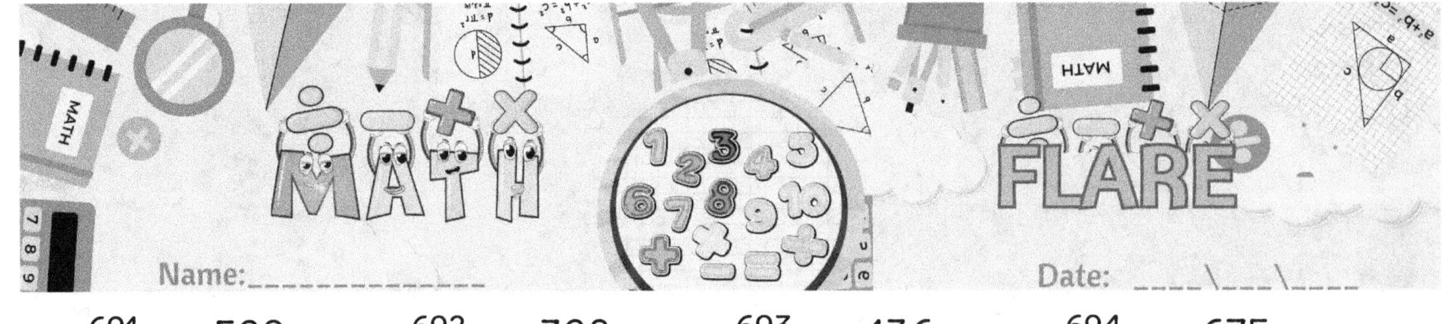

691. 529 601 + 727	692. 328 527 + 207	693. 136 172 + 414	694. 675 314 + 642
695. 382 268 + 915	696. 715 755 + 228	697. 840 577 + 763	698. 572 129 + 334
699. 163 498 + 305	700. 815 328 + 928	701. 484 645 + 340	702. 574 450 + 979
703. 404 911 + 363	704. 708 683 + 325	705. 113 288 + 244	706. 948 709 + 821

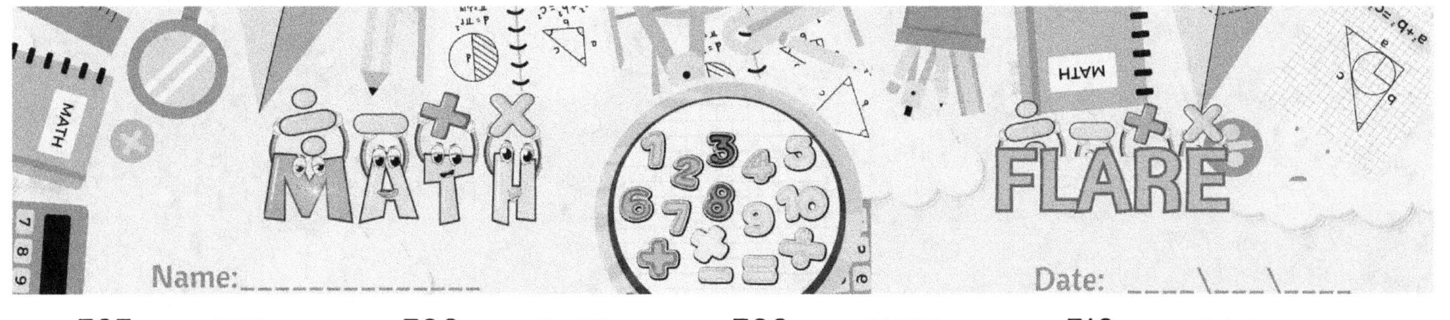

707. 771 907 + 569	708. 845 727 + 488	709. 533 956 + 572	710. 492 265 + 129
711. 901 320 + 844	712. 485 290 + 669	713. 402 807 + 817	714. 935 411 + 843
715. 863 231 + 893	716. 538 559 + 840	717. 190 214 + 788	718. 483 144 + 420
719. 458 639 + 917	720. 851 141 + 493	721. 506 911 + 746	722. 334 806 + 463

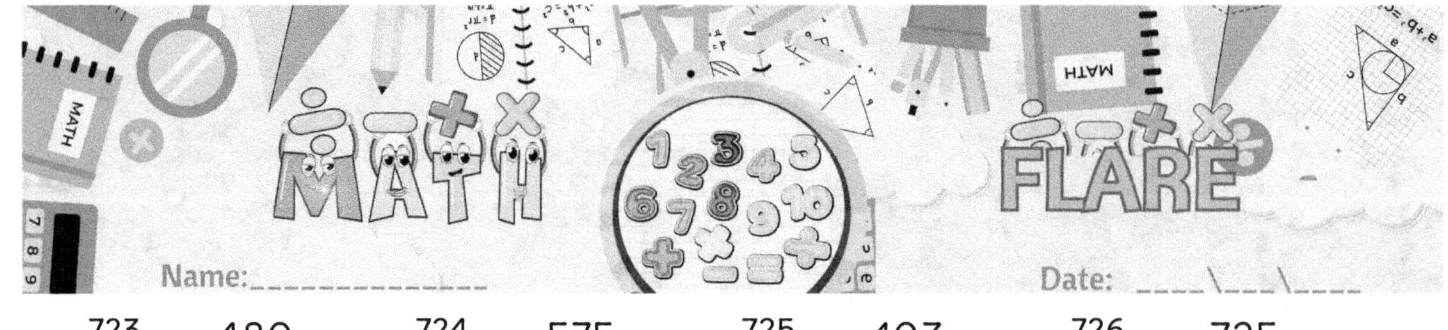

723. 480 626 + 997	724. 575 646 + 901	725. 103 834 + 596	726. 725 980 + 595
727. 594 994 + 497	728. 732 402 + 151	729. 341 518 + 276	730. 524 127 + 651
731. 751 551 + 766	732. 425 529 + 499	733. 197 629 + 424	734. 530 157 + 932
735. 842 615 + 567	736. 885 480 + 309	737. 822 733 + 657	738. 422 357 + 145

Multiple Operations: Addition Subtraction

Find the sum.

739.
```
   785
   337
 - 326
 - 226
 ______
```

740.
```
   758
 - 539
 - 152
   113
 ______
```

741.
```
   736
 - 235
 - 232
   491
 ______
```

742.
```
   912
   101
 - 517
 - 106
 ______
```

743.
```
   627
 - 239
 - 105
   665
 ______
```

744.
```
   656
 - 500
 - 150
   447
 ______
```

745.
```
   890
 - 169
   836
 - 459
 ______
```

746.
```
   725
 - 448
 - 276
   107
 ______
```

747.
```
   724
 - 399
   639
 - 283
 ______
```

748.
```
   890
   811
 - 328
 - 204
 ______
```

749.
```
   697
 - 182
   627
 - 221
 ______
```

750.
```
   801
 - 289
   342
 - 244
 ______
```

751.	752.	753.
580 - 434 - 140 567	602 477 - 140 - 385	718 205 - 335 - 239

754.	755.	756.
620 672 - 380 - 387	689 389 - 120 - 163	730 - 333 332 - 272

757.	758.	759.
910 - 454 - 206 149	686 - 378 - 272 402	948 - 323 - 427 683

760.	761.	762.
965 523 - 499 - 535	808 - 534 - 105 676	669 - 189 - 128 724

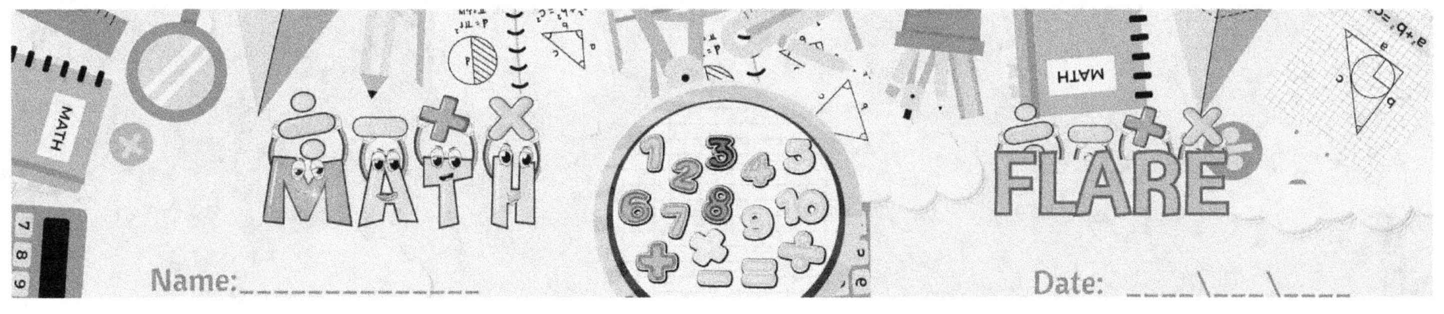

763.	764.	765.
802 - 525 961 - 206	717 - 157 926 - 347	767 - 310 - 356 398

766.	767.	768.
603 - 116 396 - 440	679 - 184 481 - 397	958 976 - 422 - 478

769.	770.	771.
744 170 - 355 - 296	768 - 377 204 - 371	871 645 - 322 - 261

772.	773.	774.
847 630 - 532 - 441	810 260 - 173 - 305	888 - 350 - 472 585

Name: _______________   Date: ____________

775.
835
- 224
415
- 135
____

776.
898
- 285
806
- 364
____

777.
652
- 152
824
- 233
____

778.
801
533
- 128
- 490
____

779.
707
- 151
- 377
563
____

780.
793
974
- 142
- 415
____

781.
650
- 399
- 112
757
____

782.
914
- 217
- 139
888
____

783.
652
125
- 460
- 145
____

784.
669
- 116
845
- 235
____

785.
918
914
- 157
- 345
____

786.
903
699
- 188
- 143
____

787.	788.	789.
600 366 - 147 - 387	972 - 249 997 - 398	630 685 - 483 - 148

790.	791.	792.
698 149 - 450 - 388	561 935 - 129 - 339	856 - 483 640 - 241

793.	794.	795.
677 - 241 725 - 386	929 - 347 923 - 352	760 985 - 376 - 331

796.	797.	798.
619 - 302 - 304 908	563 222 - 113 - 377	631 - 424 - 204 788

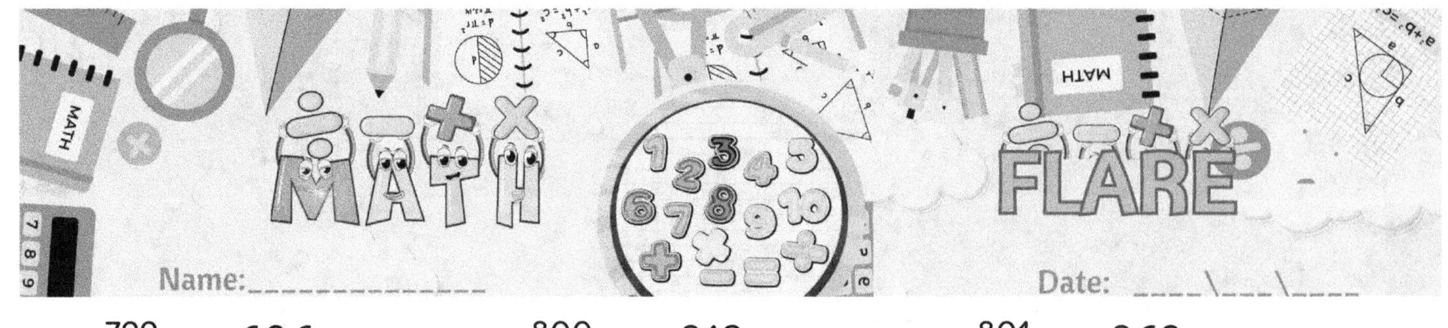

799.
```
   606
   243
 - 333
 - 457
 ______
```

800.
```
   819
 - 399
   474
 - 218
 ______
```

801.
```
   862
   811
 - 258
 - 381
 ______
```

802.
```
   836
 - 262
   839
 - 384
 ______
```

803.
```
   880
   363
 - 387
 - 255
 ______
```

804.
```
   747
   338
 - 466
 - 359
 ______
```

805.
```
   996
   250
 - 325
 - 345
 ______
```

806.
```
   920
 - 542
   217
 - 354
 ______
```

807.
```
   704
   937
 - 329
 - 407
 ______
```

808.
```
   562
   152
 - 532
 - 166
 ______
```

809.
```
   805
   417
 - 468
 - 264
 ______
```

810.
```
   592
   379
 - 217
 - 401
 ______
```

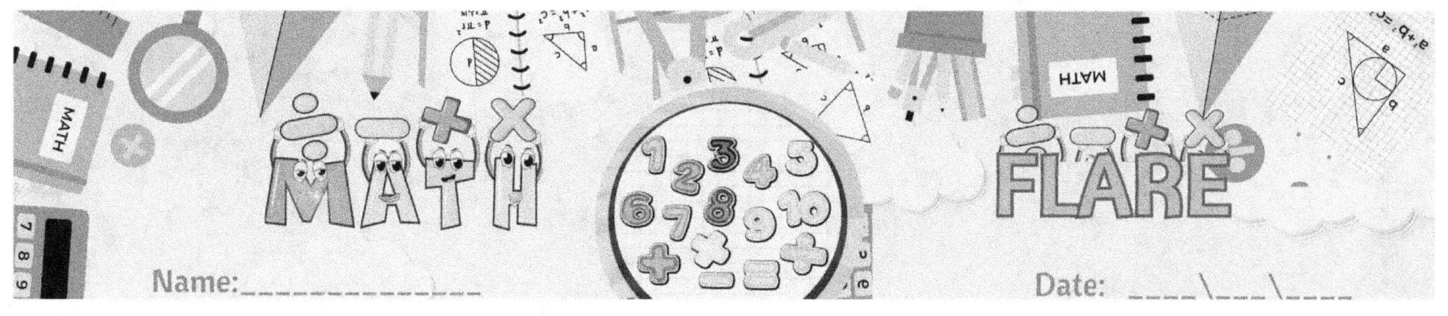

811.	812.	813.
690	585	704
− 278	662	947
− 376	− 246	− 488
901	− 488	− 294

814.	815.	816.
622	846	932
− 491	809	223
− 114	− 226	− 370
740	− 418	− 404

817.	818.	819.
699	750	958
− 476	503	847
800	− 316	− 203
− 139	− 406	− 291

820.	821.	822.
594	821	636
− 208	681	− 337
535	− 252	− 227
− 423	− 140	728

823.
```
   960
 - 147
   735
 - 238
 ______
```

824.
```
   562
   597
 - 469
 - 179
 ______
```

825.
```
   907
 - 192
 - 351
   319
 ______
```

826.
```
   930
 - 206
 - 287
   907
 ______
```

827.
```
   756
   264
 - 336
 - 249
 ______
```

828.
```
   837
   113
 - 374
 - 288
 ______
```

829.
```
   686
 - 352
 - 124
   283
 ______
```

830.
```
   909
   560
 - 316
 - 462
 ______
```

831.
```
   637
   171
 - 178
 - 253
 ______
```

832.
```
   884
 - 177
   686
 - 259
 ______
```

833.
```
   553
   148
 - 383
 - 296
 ______
```

834.
```
   856
   315
 - 492
 - 265
 ______
```

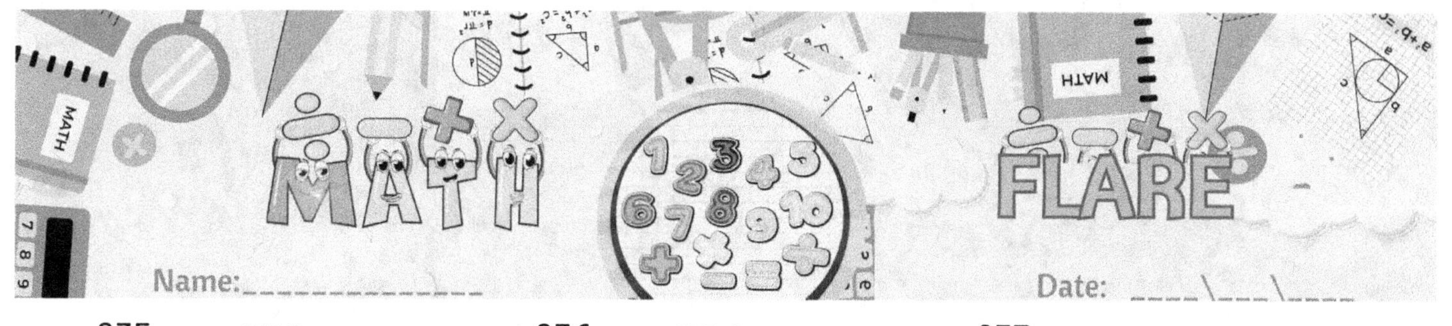

835.
652
496
- 382
- 105

836.
550
375
- 126
- 503

837.
772
- 228
- 101
520

838.
752
- 377
439
- 227

839.
875
- 438
142
- 445

840.
576
- 133
238
- 229

841.
788
- 177
- 245
626

842.
722
743
- 431
- 129

843.
860
- 430
976
- 261

844.
947
- 311
- 461
901

845.
558
- 225
860
- 305

846.
625
265
- 506
- 212

847.
```
   854
 - 255
 - 177
   936
 ______
```

848.
```
   635
 - 147
 - 218
   239
 ______
```

849.
```
   678
   405
 - 315
 - 474
 ______
```

850.
```
   992
 - 313
 - 330
   802
 ______
```

851.
```
   796
 - 521
   800
 - 422
 ______
```

852.
```
   838
 - 108
 - 280
   327
 ______
```

853.
```
   977
   240
 - 435
 - 452
 ______
```

854.
```
   652
 - 413
   207
 - 220
 ______
```

855.
```
   669
   936
 - 508
 - 117
 ______
```

856.
```
   793
 - 463
 - 301
   625
 ______
```

857.
```
   742
 - 468
 - 112
   588
 ______
```

858.
```
   996
 - 537
   916
 - 345
 ______
```

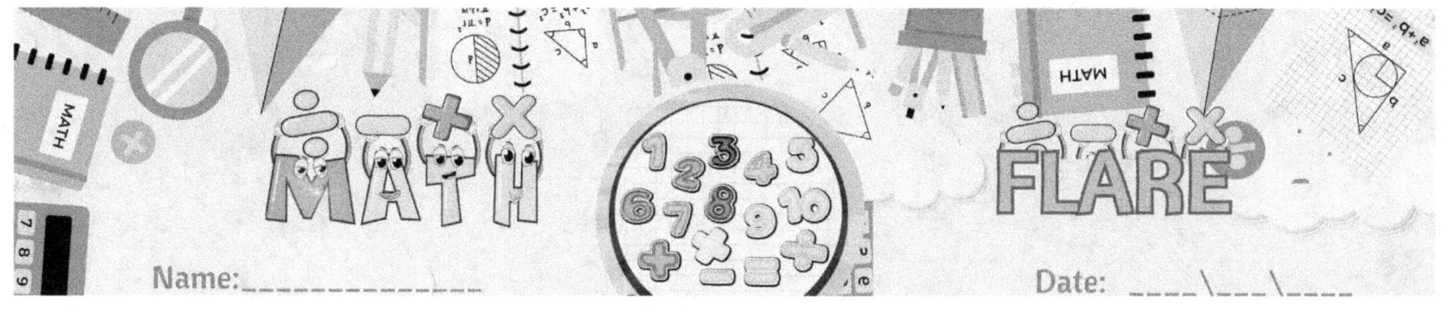

859.   894
      158
 −   508
 −   202
 ____
	860. 731
	      268
	 − 438
	 − 396
	 _______
		861. 975
		 − 513
		 − 455
		      132
		 _______

862.   711
      569
 −   516
 −   364
 ____
	863. 648
	 − 159
	      606
	 − 124
	 _______
		864. 804
		      526
		 − 207
		 − 433
		 _______

865.   577
      274
 −   229
 −   470
 ____
	866. 975
	      872
	 − 217
	 − 540
	 _______
		867. 661
		 − 189
		 − 107
		      248
		 _______

868.   905
      899
 −   523
 −   136
 ____
	869. 628
	 − 212
	      184
	 − 380
	 _______
		870. 923
		 − 477
		 − 177
		      916
		 _______

871.
```
   952
-  317
   390
-  486
―――――
```

872.
```
   732
   868
-  541
-  231
―――――
```

873.
```
   921
   250
-  175
-  195
―――――
```

874.
```
   954
   936
-  420
-  139
―――――
```

875.
```
   845
   998
-  454
-  172
―――――
```

876.
```
   775
   783
-  459
-  249
―――――
```

877.
```
   634
-  317
   889
-  241
―――――
```

878.
```
   720
-  376
-  322
   303
―――――
```

879.
```
   986
   442
-  517
-  308
―――――
```

880.
```
   790
   462
-  357
-  277
―――――
```

881.
```
   647
-  427
-  140
   660
―――――
```

882.
```
   874
   757
-  181
-  211
―――――
```

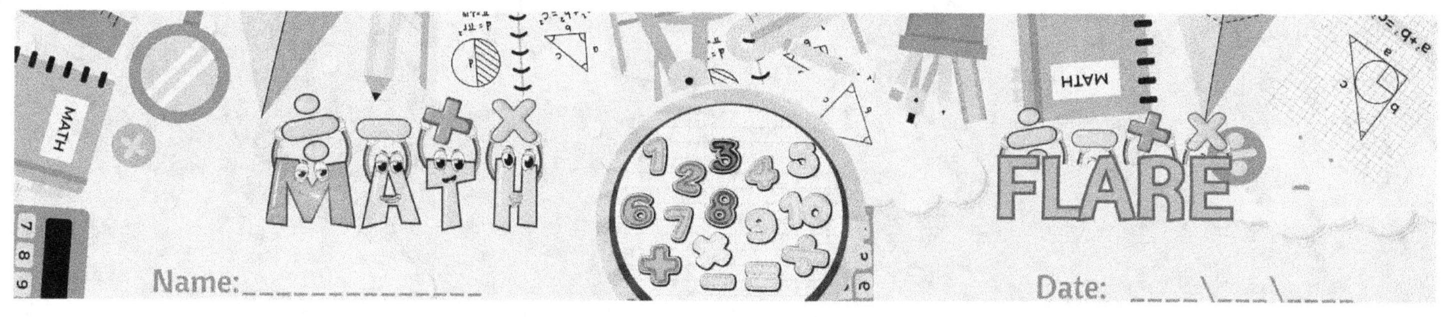

883. 791 – 103 969 – 474 ————	884. 571 – 128 – 239 221 ————	885. 857 – 545 – 242 933 ————
886. 989 – 399 – 510 291 ————	887. 665 946 – 209 – 333 ————	888. 549 323 – 348 – 208 ————
889. 741 452 – 523 – 448 ————	890. 738 – 179 649 – 306 ————	891. 684 667 – 449 – 267 ————
892. 841 – 135 – 178 914 ————	893. 989 813 – 450 – 344 ————	894. 879 681 – 288 – 348 ————

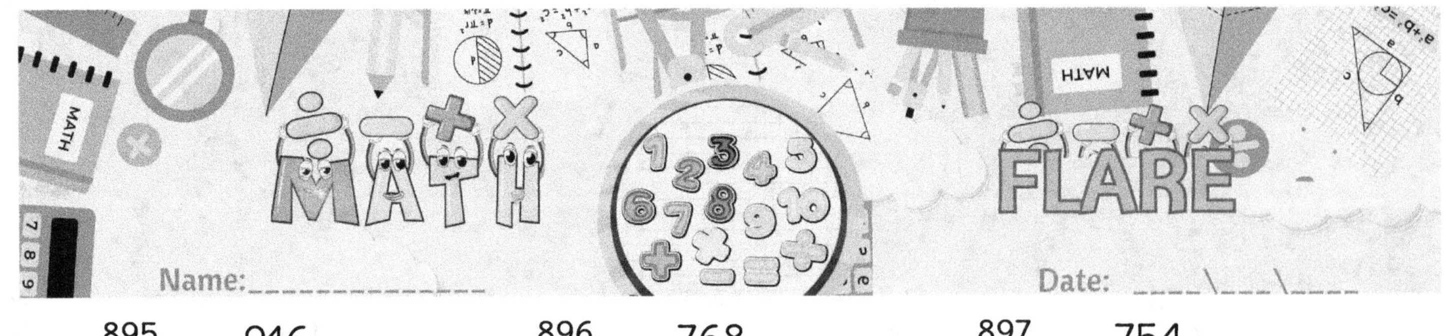

895.	916	896.	768	897.	754
	213		− 398		740
	− 264		320		− 282
	− 451		− 230		− 396

898.	604	899.	720	900.	949
	− 383		− 194		− 343
	742		662		608
	− 328		− 255		− 180

901.	894	902.	760	903.	987
	403		106		449
	− 344		− 334		− 531
	− 194		− 438		− 232

904.	914	905.	723	906.	852
	847		538		564
	− 537		− 512		− 452
	− 387		− 521		− 256

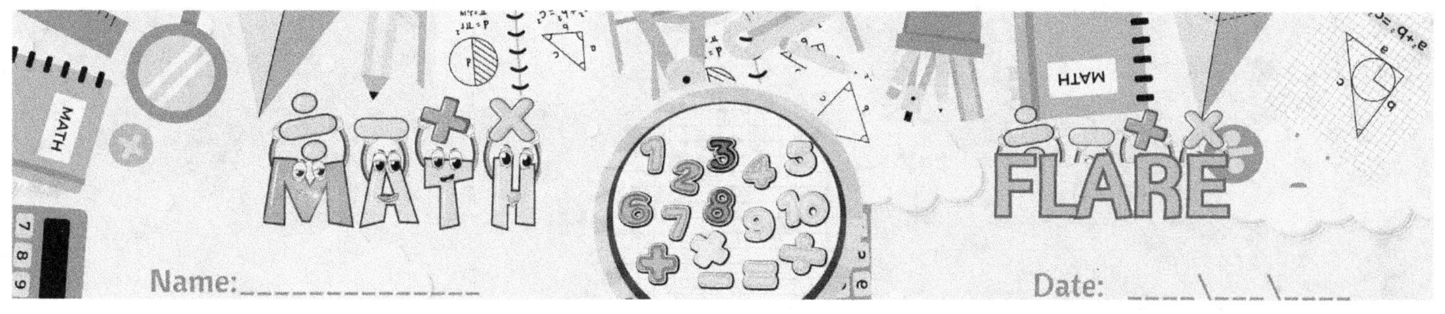

907.	908.	909.
584	558	802
343	165	- 183
- 174	- 399	113
- 334	- 161	- 167

910.	911.	912.
602	634	850
131	- 380	- 288
- 469	- 206	727
- 173	759	- 346

913.	914.	915.
656	830	798
987	- 382	275
- 531	555	- 159
- 280	- 212	- 189

916.	917.	918.
929	875	916
- 549	- 408	- 469
783	- 370	- 280
- 504	661	415

919.	920.	921.
849	923	807
− 311	− 122	− 377
771	710	− 193
− 121	− 396	131
———	———	———

922.	923.	924.
600	855	956
− 218	− 444	− 379
− 284	637	644
939	− 515	− 185
———	———	———

925.	926.	927.
939	858	759
− 453	165	647
108	− 429	− 430
− 543	− 288	− 169
———	———	———

928.	929.	930.
947	782	872
511	525	751
− 288	− 382	− 453
− 326	− 202	− 307
———	———	———

ANSWERS

Page 1: Addition with Regrouping

1. 1,310	2. 1,530	3. 1,128	4. 1,310	5. 1,313	6. 1,110
7. 1,113	8. 1,845	9. 1,251	10. 1,123	11. 1,310	12. 1,118
13. 1,122	14. 1,411	15. 1,115	16. 1,135	17. 1,912	18. 1,238
19. 1,836	20. 1,445	21. 1,112	22. 1,320	23. 1,241	24. 1,420
25. 1,617	26. 1,153	27. 1,516	28. 1,110	29. 1,211	30. 1,522
31. 1,355	32. 1,414	33. 1,822	34. 1,133	35. 1,711	36. 1,112
37. 1,210	38. 1,282	39. 1,460	40. 1,610	41. 1,120	42. 1,312
43. 1,410	44. 1,210	45. 1,313	46. 1,710	47. 1,113	48. 1,215
49. 1,241	50. 1,210	51. 1,445	52. 1,111	53. 1,112	54. 1,272
55. 1,112	56. 1,350	57. 1,465	58. 1,170	59. 1,115	60. 1,176
61. 1,212	62. 1,710	63. 1,310	64. 1,170	65. 1,116	66. 1,611
67. 1,154	68. 1,311	69. 1,460	70. 1,153	71. 1,161	72. 1,825
73. 1,550	74. 1,241	75. 1,231	76. 1,210	77. 1,110	78. 1,213
79. 1,273	80. 1,211	81. 1,235	82. 1,455	83. 1,516	84. 1,326
85. 1,550	86. 1,215	87. 1,620	88. 1,723	89. 1,131	90. 1,620
91. 1,311	92. 1,314	93. 1,217	94. 1,274	95. 1,975	96. 1,310
97. 1,213	98. 1,740	99. 1,220	100. 1,310		

Page 6: Subtraction with Regrouping

101. 36	102. 789	103. 76	104. 384	105. 278	106. 88

107. 78   108. 388   109. 87   110. 253   111. 178   112. 88

113. 283   114. 179   115. 485   116. 359   117. 16   118. 89

119. 37   120. 88   121. 45   122. 176   123. 146   124. 67

125. 389   126. 39   127. 81   128. 379   129. 189   130. 544

131. 79   132. 49   133. 77   134. 69   135. 568   136. 266

137. 175   138. 41   139. 87   140. 79   141. 168   142. 68

143. 32   144. 188   145. 283   146. 69   147. 784   148. 527

149. 72   150. 169   151. 89   152. 89   153. 584   154. 88

155. 756   156. 187   157. 86   158. 169   159. 79   160. 219

161. 75   162. 483   163. 74   164. 88   165. 38   166. 84

167. 79   168. 187   169. 176   170. 88   171. 88   172. 338

173. 89   174. 389   175. 459   176. 78   177. 68   178. 86

179. 89   180. 79   181. 353   182. 106   183. 58   184. 387

185. 83   186. 86   187. 38   188. 289   189. 29   190. 87

191. 47   192. 87   193. 129   194. 71   195. 79   196. 87

197. 476   198. 189   199. 68   200. 387

Page 11: Addition - Doubles

201. 1,497   202. 1,572   203. 593   204. 650   205. 224

206. 848   207. 1,880   208. 1,508   209. 787   210. 1,496

211. 839   212. 1,647   213. 1,523   214. 1,070   215. 1,278

216. 392   217. 1,412   218. 1,718   219. 1,132   220. 1,282

221. 257	222. 1,538	223. 391	224. 408	225. 386
226. 874	227. 838	228. 424	229. 1,701	230. 1,151
231. 943	232. 932	233. 1,184	234. 865	235. 1,682
236. 1,574	237. 565	238. 1,023	239. 1,213	240. 883
241. 1,158	242. 1,991	243. 1,352	244. 212	245. 367
246. 919	247. 336	248. 910	249. 214	250. 662
251. 347	252. 367	253. 1,988	254. 1,280	255. 1,731
256. 1,815	257. 271	258. 482	259. 850	260. 1,064
261. 1,636	262. 1,475	263. 1,997	264. 478	265. 491
266. 640	267. 1,737	268. 1,093	269. 1,372	270. 1,852
271. 232	272. 1,243	273. 819	274. 1,982	275. 1,505
276. 892	277. 891	278. 1,121	279. 1,268	280. 1,957
281. 1,946	282. 936	283. 808	284. 1,217	285. 810
286. 223	287. 1,492	288. 1,524	289. 1,663	290. 520
291. 532	292. 1,734	293. 985	294. 440	295. 1,479
296. 382	297. 1,436	298. 1,402	299. 250	300. 507

Page 16: Addition Unknown Number

301. 88	302. 14	303. 75	304. 48	305. 11	306. 59
307. 93	308. 72	309. 66	310. 122	311. 75	312. 154
313. 121	314. 161	315. 44	316. 110	317. 17	318. 99
319. 150	320. 130	321. 66	322. 95	323. 9	324. 114

325. 120   326. 61   327. 46   328. 151   329. 66   330. 112

331. 15   332. 153   333. 29   334. 38   335. 132   336. 120

337. 131   338. 44   339. 136   340. 74   341. 141   342. 21

343. 65   344. 112   345. 64   346. 34   347. 100   348. 66

349. 113   350. 97   351. 14   352. 110   353. 120   354. 170

355. 114   356. 16   357. 94   358. 110   359. 163   360. 15

361. 76   362. 7   363. 35   364. 65   365. 99   366. 12

367. 58   368. 28   369. 73   370. 21   371. 41   372. 1

373. 130   374. 64   375. 181   376. 78   377. 18   378. 69

379. 61   380. 117   381. 71   382. 49   383. 86   384. 51

385. 27   386. 88   387. 135   388. 9

Page 21: Subtraction: Unknown Number

389. 28   390. 10   391. 96   392. 23   393. 55   394. 27   395. 68

396. 51   397. 27   398. 28   399. 89   400. 32   401. 1   402. 16

403. 35   404. 21   405. 18   406. 54   407. 20   408. 49   409. 24

410. 54   411. 58   412. 12   413. 23   414. 0   415. 2   416. 95

417. 49   418. 31   419. 41   420. 30   421. 19   422. 91   423. 31

424. 2   425. 12   426. 27   427. 33   428. 18   429. 83   430. 66

431. 6   432. 98   433. 25   434. 41   435. 48   436. 63   437. 76

438. 13   439. 35   440. 42   441. 57   442. 55   443. 28   444. 57

445. 11   446. 21   447. 72   448. 38   449. 87   450. 11   451. 39

452. 97   453. 9   454. 87   455. 70   456. 1   457. 39   458. 36

459. 9   460. 9   461. 32   462. 41   463. 25   464. 32   465. 8

466. 1   467. 34   468. 44   469. 53   470. 38   471. 53   472. 15

473. 20   474. 81   475. 66   476. 42

Page 26: Make 1000

477. 309   478. 115   479. 995   480. 622   481. 542   482. 195

483. 147   484. 250   485. 786   486. 273   487. 289   488. 343

489. 14   490. 648   491. 606   492. 10   493. 996   494. 71

495. 142   496. 519   497. 64   498. 974   499. 745   500. 743

501. 951   502. 589   503. 176   504. 320   505. 518   506. 141

507. 328   508. 670   509. 74   510. 150   511. 144   512. 63

513. 224   514. 409   515. 507   516. 386   517. 479   518. 489

519. 548   520. 139   521. 21   522. 582   523. 940   524. 605

525. 441   526. 948   527. 672   528. 886   529. 552   530. 238

531. 898   532. 994   533. 43   534. 427   535. 431   536. 428

537. 267   538. 804   539. 461   540. 677   541. 175   542. 49

543. 591   544. 628   545. 537   546. 880

Page 30: Addition (3 Addends)

547. 2,210   548. 1,628   549. 1,239   550. 1,963   551. 2,099

552. 1,784   553. 2,589   554. 2,150   555. 1,303   556. 2,126

557. 1,964   558. 1,834   559. 2,115   560. 1,820   561. 703

562. 1,957   563. 2,473   564. 1,531   565. 1,936   566. 2,049

567. 2,407   568. 1,661   569. 1,480   570. 1,790   571. 1,710

572. 1,287   573. 1,505   574. 2,209   575. 2,155   576. 1,900

577. 1,525   578. 876   579. 2,449   580. 2,147   581. 1,745

582. 728   583. 1,641   584. 1,759   585. 1,260   586. 1,721

587. 1,942   588. 1,345   589. 1,608   590. 1,823   591. 1,893

592. 1,755   593. 1,537   594. 2,216   595. 1,811   596. 1,772

597. 1,493   598. 1,676   599. 2,401   600. 1,311   601. 2,290

602. 1,900   603. 1,507   604. 1,685   605. 1,052   606. 1,417

607. 2,181   608. 1,546   609. 1,373   610. 1,869   611. 1,549

612. 1,926   613. 1,335   614. 1,332   615. 1,574   616. 2,656

617. 1,877   618. 2,018   619. 1,664   620. 2,204   621. 1,434

622. 1,771   623. 1,464   624. 1,874   625. 1,800   626. 1,404

627. 1,461   628. 1,672   629. 2,193   630. 1,526   631. 2,152

632. 1,446   633. 2,062   634. 1,786   635. 977   636. 1,546

637. 911   638. 1,064   639. 1,258   640. 2,079   641. 1,859

642. 1,818   643. 2,335   644. 1,943   645. 1,150   646. 1,991

647. 1,364   648. 1,315   649. 1,405   650. 1,471   651. 1,280

652. 1,166   653. 2,035   654. 1,149   655. 2,130   656. 907

657. 1,890   658. 856   659. 1,590   660. 1,856   661. 1,966

662. 2,009   663. 1,142   664. 1,062   665. 906   666. 1,550

667. 1,186   668. 2,111   669. 1,372   670. 693   671. 1,336

672. 1,049   673. 1,796   674. 1,857   675. 1,623   676. 1,428

677. 1,391   678. 2,468   679. 1,356   680. 2,239   681. 1,288

682. 1,562   683. 1,290   684. 1,592   685. 1,845   686. 1,543

687. 1,913   688. 2,667   689. 1,920   690. 1,829   691. 1,857

692. 1,062   693. 722   694. 1,631   695. 1,565   696. 1,698

697. 2,180   698. 1,035   699. 966   700. 2,071   701. 1,469

702. 2,003   703. 1,678   704. 1,716   705. 645   706. 2,478

707. 2,247   708. 2,060   709. 2,061   710. 886   711. 2,065

712. 1,444   713. 2,026   714. 2,189   715. 1,987   716. 1,937

717. 1,192   718. 1,047   719. 2,014   720. 1,485   721. 2,163

722. 1,603   723. 2,103   724. 2,122   725. 1,533   726. 2,300

727. 2,085   728. 1,285   729. 1,135   730. 1,302   731. 2,068

732. 1,453   733. 1,250   734. 1,619   735. 2,024   736. 1,674

737. 2,212   738. 924

Page 42: Multiple Operations: Addition Subtraction

739. 570   740. 180   741. 760   742. 390   743. 948

744. 453   745. 1,098   746. 108   747. 681   748. 1,169

749. 921   750. 610   751. 573   752. 554   753. 349

754. 525   755. 795   756. 457   757. 399   758. 438

759. 881   760. 454   761. 845   762. 1,076   763. 1,032

764. 1,139 765. 499 766. 443 767. 579 768. 1,034
769. 263 770. 224 771. 933 772. 504 773. 592
774. 651 775. 891 776. 1,055 777. 1,091 778. 716
779. 742 780. 1,210 781. 896 782. 1,446 783. 172
784. 1,163 785. 1,330 786. 1,271 787. 432 788. 1,322
789. 684 790. 9 791. 1,028 792. 772 793. 775
794. 1,153 795. 1,038 796. 921 797. 295 798. 791
799. 59 800. 676 801. 1,034 802. 1,029 803. 601
804. 260 805. 576 806. 241 807. 905 808. 16
809. 490 810. 353 811. 937 812. 513 813. 869
814. 757 815. 1,011 816. 381 817. 884 818. 531
819. 1,311 820. 498 821. 1,110 822. 800 823. 1,310
824. 511 825. 683 826. 1,344 827. 435 828. 288
829. 493 830. 691 831. 377 832. 1,134 833. 22
834. 414 835. 661 836. 296 837. 963 838. 587
839. 134 840. 452 841. 992 842. 905 843. 1,145
844. 1,076 845. 888 846. 172 847. 1,358 848. 509
849. 294 850. 1,151 851. 653 852. 777 853. 330
854. 226 855. 980 856. 654 857. 750 858. 1,030
859. 342 860. 165 861. 139 862. 400 863. 971
864. 690 865. 152 866. 1,090 867. 613 868. 1,145

869. 220   870. 1,185   871. 539   872. 828   873. 801

874. 1,331   875. 1,217   876. 850   877. 965   878. 325

879. 603   880. 618   881. 740   882. 1,239   883. 1,183

884. 425   885. 1,003   886. 371   887. 1,069   888. 316

889. 222   890. 902   891. 635   892. 1,442   893. 1,008

894. 924   895. 414   896. 460   897. 816   898. 635

899. 933   900. 1,034   901. 759   902. 94   903. 673

904. 837   905. 228   906. 708   907. 419   908. 163

909. 565   910. 91   911. 807   912. 943   913. 832

914. 791   915. 725   916. 659   917. 758   918. 582

919. 1,188   920. 1,115   921. 368   922. 1,037   923. 533

924. 1,036   925. 51   926. 306   927. 807   928. 844

929. 723   930. 863